The Smilin'

—— featuring Eleanor Dahl ——

EIGHT MILES NORTH

...and one mile
east of Wroxton

Published by
farringtonmedia

in co-operation with

TRAFFORD

Note for Librarians: A cataloguing record for this book is available from Library and Archives Canada at www.collectionscanada.ca/amicus/index-e.html
ISBN 1-4120-8912-3

Printed in Victoria, BC, Canada. Printed on paper with minimum 30% recycled fibre. Trafford's print shop runs on "green energy" from solar, wind and other environmentally-friendly power sources.

TRAFFORD
PUBLISHING™

Offices in Canada, USA, Ireland and UK

Book sales for North America and international:
Trafford Publishing, 6E–2333 Government St.,
Victoria, BC V8T 4P4 CANADA
phone 250 383 6864 (toll-free 1 888 232 4444)
fax 250 383 6804; email to orders@trafford.com

Book sales in Europe:
Trafford Publishing (UK) Limited, 9 Park End Street, 2nd Floor
Oxford, UK OX1 1HH UNITED KINGDOM
phone +44 (0)1865 722 113 (local rate 0845 230 9601)
facsimile +44 (0)1865 722 868; info.uk@trafford.com

Order online at:
trafford.com/06-0668

10 9 8 7 6 5 4

Message From: *Smilin' Johnnie Eleanor Dahl*

Smilin' Johnnie Shows
Box 190-210
Wroxton, Saskatchewan S0A 4S0
Phone: 1(306) 742-4356

Dearest Friend:

We have entered into our **60th YEAR** in music, and within those years, your life has touched ours in such a way that we count you as our friends.

You have helped us in a unique way that enabled us to carry on all those years, entertaining folks throughout our country.

Through many of those years it was difficult to carry on--Friend, you have no idea how your assistance helped us through. Your help may have seemed minuscule to you, but it was enough to make a HUGE difference to us.

The BOOK, the CD's, the CASSETTES, and ALL personal appearances were done with YOUR help. My wife and I take this opportunity to thank GOD and FRIENDS like you for this help--and may GOD richly bless you.

Thank you very much--

Sincerely yours,

Johnnie & Eleanor

PASS THE WORD

"Always Have A Good Day"

DEDICATION

I am dedicating this story of my life to the people who mean the most to me - my children and their loved ones. There were times when I wish that we could have spent more time together. I love you all.

My son Jerry and his wife Sue and their daughter Rachel

My son Bobby, his wife Cheri and their daughter Morgan (her fiancée David Dean) and son Zachary

My son John, his wife Kim

My daughter Tamara and her husband Doug

My late infant daughter Marie who was taken from us too soon

TABLE OF CONTENTS

TABLE OF CONTENTS

TABLE OF CONTENTS

Some of the words to songs Smilin' Johnnie and Eleanor have written and recorded:

ACKNOWLEDGMENTS

I would especially like to thank people who have helped me and made a difference in my life:

- Eddie and Lorraine Achtemichuk for their help with promotion and design and creation of CD covers and video covers.

- Glen McDougall, of Fury Electric Instruments, guitar-maker extra-ordinaire who - as a special favour - did all the artwork for our eight LP album covers. Some of these are on display Brock Silverside's museum in Medicine Hat.

- John Farrington, the editor who helped me get my thoughts and writings arranged for this book

Eddie and Lorraine
Achtemichuk

- All those in small-town Canada who booked us into their community halls over the years

- Lawrence and Dot Zelionka for their friendship and help all along the way.

- The genuine people of this country of all creeds and colours who welcomed us with open arms into their culture and their life . . . and made us feel good about what we were doing

- And I will always be thankful to Mom and Dad Lucki for their support and for giving us our little piece of heaven on earth.

Publication design: farringtonmedia. Oakville
Cover design: www.ANDREWtheARTIST.com, Brussels, Belgium

Published by
farringtonmedia

2007 Erika Court
Oakville, Ontario, Canada, L6M 4R4
Tel,. 905-469-4201 Fax: 905-469-4202
email: john@farringtonmedia.com
www.farringtonmedia,com
in co-operation with

TRAFFORD

6E - 2333 Government Street
Victoria, B.C., Canada, V8T 4P4
www.trafford.com

Smilin' Johnnie

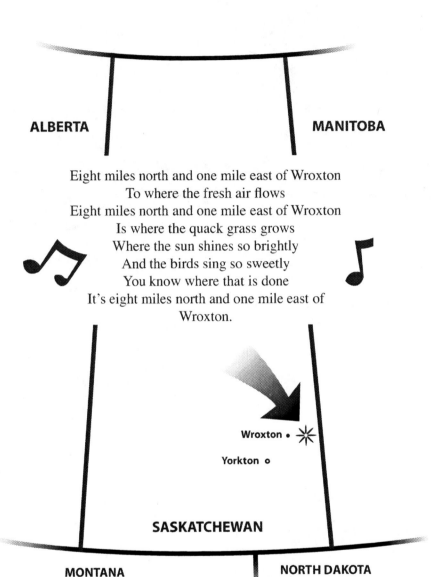

Eight miles north and one mile east of Wroxton
To where the fresh air flows
Eight miles north and one mile east of Wroxton
Is where the quack grass grows
Where the sun shines so brightly
And the birds sing so sweetly
You know where that is done
It's eight miles north and one mile east of
Wroxton.

ALBERTA

MANITOBA

Wroxton •

Yorkton o

SASKATCHEWAN

MONTANA

NORTH DAKOTA

INTRODUCTION

Smilin' Johnnie. You've probably never heard of him. But he's spent a lifetime in the Canadian music industry.

Some of that has to do with the fact that he put himself in a kind of time warp. He decided way back – and I'm talking in the late 1940s - that Nashville was not the place for him and his group.

He didn't like the sound of the new country music – and I don't mean the Garth Brooks and the Shania Twains. Way back when the twang of the old country music switched to a more truckers and lovers sound with the early Johnny Cash.

It was at this time, in the early 1950s, that Elvis Presley started wrigglin' and writhin' and rock and roll was being born.

Smilin' Johnnie tried it. Didn't like it. Confirmed himself a pure country singer, like his favourite Ernest Tubb, standing up straight as a die at the microphone, dressed in the most sequined and patriotic stage costumes of the early pioneers of country music.

No jeans. No plaid shirts. He goes back to a time when entertainers would dress up to go on stage. It was a uniform. Usually everyone in the group would dress the same.

It is an era long since gone, except for Smilin' Johnnie. Single-handedly, he's kept it alive. This is a music and a time that he won't let die. It's the late 40s and early 50s. The Second World War had just ended. The country was getting back on its feet after the better part of a decade of horror.

He's been true to himself over the years.

He's had his 15 minutes of fame a number of times over: he's written to politicians to try to get them to change the Canadian music industry and protect it from the controlling interests of the United States . . . how many Canadian entertainers have been discussed in the Canadian Parliament and had their names recorded in Hansard?

Smilin' Johnnie has recorded more than 50 LPs, cassettes and CDs – many with just the simplest of equipment in his basement in front of a mike - but he's never had a hit record. Over the years they have sold a total of about 5,000 LPs, tapes or cassettes.

Introduction

Smilin' Johnnie has played in thousands of halls and community centres across Canada. He doesn't play the regular theatres, or arenas, and often is not on a stage. Some of the halls have pull-out risers, but that's it.

Many entertainers will say they have played "all over Canada" but, says Smilin' Johnnie, "what they mean is they have played Halifax, Montreal, Toronto, Ottawa, Winnipeg. Regina, Calgary, Vancouver."

When Smilin' Johnnnie says he has played all over Canada he really means it. He's played in small communities that tourists don't get to see.

He's travelled more than seven million miles (11,625,408 kilometres) by all modes of transport from trains to airplanes, boat to dog-team, snowmobile, car, gas truck and even a funeral home limo.

He has spent an entire lifetime entertaining the people of Canada. Smilin' Johnnie and his wife, Eleanor Dahl have been on the road together for 45 years. Johnnie started professionally 15 years before that!

Sixty years in show business and still going strong.

He has never sought fame. His wife says he has always preferred a house full of friends to a bank account full of money.

Smilin' Johnnie and Eleanor are the most genuine people you'd ever want to meet.

They could be anyone's grandparents.

They own 40 acres of land *Eight Miles North and One Mile East of Wroxton,* Saskatchewan. And for those of you who have never heard of Wroxton – with its post office, grain elevator and couple of dozen houses - it is about 40 kilometres east of Yorkton.

It's in the parkland of Saskatchewan, 150 kilometers from the famous prairie land, where they both grew up and love so much.

Their home is one mile off the beaten track of the road to Kamsack. It is nestled in a clump of trees, protected (a little bit, anyway) from the howling winter winds that sometimes can dump a foot of snow overnight.

Smilin' Johnnie and Eleanor not only sing songs like they used to sound long ago in the good ol' days before rock 'n' roll swept the land, they live like it is the 1940s, too. Their little wooden bungalow, painted in one-foot-wide black and white horizontal stripes, is NOT insulated. They don't have indoor plumbing. Floor covering is one-foot-square pieces of linoleum salvaged from discarded samples – and it doesn't matter if they match, it is a patchwork of patterns.

They don't have doors on any rooms in the house – just a curtain on their bedroom and another in the bathroom, where Eleanor has her own composting toilet, a lot more modern and comfortable than Johnnie's personal pail.

They don't have a dish washer. Eleanor does all the dishes by hand. Their television is no bigger than 15 inches and sits on a filing cabinet in Smilin' Johnnie's office. They view it from the living room through the office doorway. There is just no room for the television, even as small and portable as it is, in the living room that is filled with mementoes of their travels.

They are simple, down to earth folk. Genuine to a fault. Delightful in many ways, frugal in every way.

I say all of this because neither Smilin' Johnnie, nor Eleanor would ever say it. They love the life they lead. They love life period. They don't see anything extra-ordinary about how they live. They have always lived this way.

Smilin' Johnnie and Eleanor didn't have running water when they moved onto the property that was given to them by Johnnie's dad when he was still alive. He had 80 acres in his will for them, but when they started looking to buy property about 40 years ago he said that he didn't have to die to give it to them.

They sold off 40 acres and have lived happily on the property ever since.

They have electricity and they have a telephone line – with a phone in every room in the house – but they are so far off the beaten track they are not hooked up to municipal water and sewer.

They used the proceeds from one show about 30 years ago to dig a well on their property to get running water. Before that, once a week, he'd fill the station wagon with nine five-gallon pails of water from his parents house in Wroxton. The municipality found out about the water trips and they started billing him $60 a year for the water.

Today the only service he receives from the municipality is snowplowing in the winter – usually two or three days after a major storm when all other roads have been plowed, and grading and gravelling the off-the-beaten path 'road' to his house in the summer.

His total municipal taxes in 2005 were $234. That's for the year. Not a monthly charge.

Introduction

Smilin' Johnnie and Eleanor are church-goers with moral standards that befit the era they portray – the 1940s. They are people who don't smoke, drink socially, swear only in dire circumstances, don't care for off-colour jokes, and are as devoted to each other as any two people could be.

While they choose to live the way they do, they are well aware of the world today, thanks to their favourite television news program every night at 10 p.m., The National with Peter Mansbridge.

It has been – and continues to be - an interesting life for Smilin' Johnnie and Eleanor. This book won't get into the sex and sleaze that often has a habit of clinging to the entertainers of our day. Other than to record, as a matter of life, there's no dwelling on the fact Smilin' Johnnie was married twice, and Eleanor once, before they fell in love with each other.

They are happy-go-lucky (pun intended, Johnnie's surname is Lucky). They embrace life. Respect each other . . . very much in the traditional sense where the man does all the heavy work (even climbing on the roof to fix things and clear snow in his 80s) and the woman does all the cooking, the cleaning, the dusting. Just another throwback to that time warp they live in and perform in.

Smilin' Johnnie and Eleanor are a really entertaining and engaging couple with a lot of fascinating stories to tell. Enjoy.

John Farrington

Editor and Publisher

March 2006

John Farrington has been a journalist for 48 years, starting in his English hometown weekly in Crewe, Cheshire, in July 1958. He worked in England for seven years before emigrating to Canada in 1965. He has been Managing Editor at several Canadian newspapers, including Kirkland Lake, Peterborough, Sarnia, Lethbridge, and Sudbury and Publisher and General Manager in Nanaimo, Timmins. Cornwall and the Multicom group in Toronto. He was National Editorial Consultant for Thomson Newspapers from 1980-1982 and Northern Ontario Journalist of the Year in 1990. He collaborated with Stompin' Tom Connors on his Number 1 autobiography. Currently he operates his own company, farringtonmedia, editing and writing books, and produces a quarterly in-flight magazine for Air Creebec, serving the Cree communities in the James Bay area of Ontario and Quebec.

FOREWORD

By Jerry Lucky

W e've all heard the terrible stories about children raised with parents who
are entertainers. You know the kind I mean, the kids who were ignored,
or spoiled beyond belief, or those who feel they simply had a rotten childhood.
While I know this happens, I'm living proof it doesn't have to be that way. At
least it wasn't for me.

The story that unfolds on the pages that follow is the story of my father, Smilin'
Johnnie, a man who was driven to perform. From the first time he picked up
the guitar and played in front of a live audience it seems he was hooked on the
idea that he could entertain people and everybody would have a good time. It
was like a drug and he was addicted. What else could explain a person doing
what he did? Countless hours on the road, driving through the night, having to
deal with inflamed artistic egos, performing for unscrupulous promoters and
lots more you'll read about.

You would think having a dad who was on the road as much as Smilin' Johnnie
would have caused any number of problems for the children growing up in that
environment. But that just wasn't the case. Ours was a pretty normal family of
four and I was the oldest. What I remember most about growing up in a musical
family is not that dad was away a lot, but that when he was home, he was really
home. See, when dad was away, he and mom had a special phone code and dad
would make every effort to call each and every night to see how everyone was.
If the boys, that was my brother and I, had been well behaved mom and dad
might not even complete the call. But if we had misbehaved dad would know
about it. In that sense it was like he was there. We not only learned the value
of behaving responsibly, we also came to know that dad cared about us. And
just because he wasn't there each and every day like other dads, he showed us
with those phone calls that he loved us. Sometimes we would talk to him on
the phone but most times these calls were kept to a minimum because long-
distance was expensive.

I don't ever remember our family having a lot of money. But then I don't
remember us without money either. It's funny; growing up dad always made
sure we had what we needed, and even plenty of things we just wanted. Like
every other kid, I had a bike, I had toys, I had books, I had models, as far as

Foreword

I knew I had it all. Plus I had a dad whose job was interesting and exciting. Not every kid had a dad who was a musician performing on a stage in front of crowds of people.

As you would expect, there was always music around the house. Either dad was writing or rehearsing or music would be playing on the little record player we had. Records were in the mail every day and coming home from school was always exciting because you never knew what would be waiting in the mail. Lots of times I got to open the packages to see what new records had been released that week. Wow, not many kids got to do that.

Dad never said to us don't become musicians but he didn't encourage it either. He seemed to know that while it was rewarding it was also a pretty hard life with long hours and sometimes little financial reward. None-the-less it was watching dad perform his live music radio show on radio station CJNB (in North Battleford, Saskatchewan) that inspired me to choose broadcasting as a career. In Grade 6 at the age of 12. I decided that was what I wanted to do and by Grade 11 I got my first radio job on air. I continue to work in radio to this day.

Growing up with Smilin' Johnnie as my father was amazing and has given me so many memories. Like the time dad returned from a lengthy trip, driving three days straight to get home. And then while he slept we loaded up the car for a family vacation. Dad got up and we all headed on the highway to Texas for a family holiday. In fact, being in the car was almost a second home for us. We may not have had a lot of money to do stuff, but we could always get in the car and go for a drive. Many times that drive would end in a stop at some take-out restaurant. I've often reflected back on those drives as special family time, which perhaps explains why I'm always suggesting to my wife and daughter that we could just go for a drive.

By now you're thinking I must be really sugar-coating this story, but as you'll read in the pages that follow my father got up to more than his share of trouble over the years. It was a tough life, full of ups and downs. There may have been many rewarding moments, but as you can imagine there were plenty of outrageous antics too with life on the road. He's far from what some would call a "saint" and he'll be the first to admit he wasn't a perfect dad. But you know what, that was the only childhood I had and it was a pretty good one. I have no complaints and I certainly wouldn't trade my memories or experiences for anyone else's'. Warts and all, this is the story of my dad, Smilin' Johnnie.

Smilin' Johnnie

Jerry Lucky is Smilin' Johnnie's oldest son. He lives with his wife, Sue, and daughter Rachel on Vancouver Island, in Brentwood Bay, just outside of Victoria, British Columbia. He continues to work in broadcasting as a Sales Account Manager at radio station CIOC-FM. While he never became a professional musician like his father, he maintains a close involvement with music by constantly listening to it and by writing about it in books, magazines and on the internet. The musical gene instilled by his dad has certainly been passed on to his daughter Rachel as she has - at various times - wanted to play drums or guitar. However, she has settled to listening to music, much like her father – very loudly. All of this continues to baffle her mother, Sue, but she remains very accommodating.

1

Making music for 60 years

I have never worked a day in my life. And I am proud of that.   I have never received a government handout, either. And I am proud of that, too.

You see, I have spent my entire life doing something I really love – entertaining people. I am a country and western singer and have travelled more than seven million miles making people happy, even making them laugh. And that makes me feel good.

I am long past regular retirement age as I write this . . . I am 81 years-old. I have been making music professionally for 60 years. As long as I stay healthy I intend to keep entertaining.

What have I got? Five? Ten? Fifteen years? I wish.

It's been a great life. I wouldn't want it any other way. I haven't enjoyed every single second, but I have made the most of every day.

I have learned from mistakes, even paid handsomely, emotionally, for some things. But, you know, I don't look back at my life and wish that things had gone differently.

Oh, I'll be honest, there have been a couple of things that I wished would have been better. My love life was rough for a while. And one of the penalties of my second messed-up marriage was that I only got custody of the two eldest of my four children.

Smilin' Johnnie

However, I don't blame anyone but myself for that. I am an entertainer. I was travelling more than 200 days a year back then. Why would anyone in their right mind give me custody of my kids? It was tough at the time, even devastating. But I am a musician and musicians have a reputation of not setting down roots and I accepted the decision that was made as one that was best for the children. And, of course, I wanted the best for the kids. And I didn't want to cause my wife any unnecessary grief.

Being a musician didn't make things easier. Absence sure makes the heart grow fonder. I don't think a day went by without me thinking of my kids. Wondering what they were doing . . . wondering if they were thinking about me as much as I was thinking about them . . . wondering whether there ever would be a day when we might get together again . . . wondering what they would think of me when they grew up.

Not seeing my kids, when they were kids, has been heart-breaking. Even today, in quiet moments, I think about how different things might have been had I not been on the road so much. But after the tears subside I settle back and realise that life has played out the way it should. That doesn't mean I have liked everything and embraced it all. What it means is that I have had my share of excitement and my share of upsets.

But all things being equal I think that the Lord has blessed me in a wonderful way. I have been married three times. For me it was third time lucky in love and Eleanor and I have now been married 31 years.

So you can see most of the family turmoil occurred in my early years.

While my struggles in love have been difficult for me, I am sure that my first two wives and my four children had more than their fair share of tears and challenges created by me just not being there for them.

Family means a lot to me. But obviously the call of the road meant more. I chose between a wife and children and playing music that took me away from home. I don't think at a time when it mattered that I stopped to think of my life in the stark reality of actually choosing music over family. But that's what now I realise I did.

It wasn't that I didn't try to stay home. I did. I tried to be a more conventional stay-at-home get-a-real-job dad. But that just wasn't me. As much as I liked those days at home with my wife and kids, it didn't take long for the music bug to bite me again and I just couldn't resist the wanderlust that is the entertainment world.

Making music for 60 years

One thing that I have enjoyed all my life is amazing health. I never get sick. Oh, the odd cold like everyone else, and I must confess to more than a few aching, creaking bones. But here I am, almost 20 years past the normal retirement age, and everything seems to be working well.

This I can attribute to the fact that I have never allowed myself to grow old. I can't afford to, even if I did want to take it easy. And not only is the body working well, so is the mind.

I don't have staff to help with the business. I do everything myself. Always have. And at this stage in life and career I still do everything from promotion to playing. Oh, Eleanor helps. We are a great team. There's a lot more to show biz than standing on stage in fancy suits and playing a three-hour show.

We don't have roadies. We lug in our own equipment wherever we go. It's about 30 pieces and takes us both about 90 minutes to set up. We travel in a station wagon filled with speakers, microphones and instruments, tapes and CDs.

The two of us put on a three-hour show and then we take down the set and all the equipment and instruments, as well as the stage clothing, has to be fitted back in the station wagon. Then we travel home, or to the next job.

From Day 1 in the business I have been disappointed in the Canadian music industry cowtowing to the American music business. Don't get me wrong, I have no qualms about the United States. I just don't like the way Canadians feel mesmerized by the U.S. The entire music business is governed, if you will, by the American influence. No-one has ever been able to stand up to the Americans. In fact, I often wonder whether we have no one to blame but ourselves as Canadians for the sorry state of our national music business.

We have the talent in Canada. We have always had the talent. I can rhyme off a number of household names that are Canadian – Hank Snow, Wilf Carter, Michelle Wright, Shania Twain, Sarah McLaughlin, Alannis Morrisette, Avril Lavigne. A pretty amazing list of stars known the world over. All are Canadians who had to leave Canada to make it big. I don't blame them for leaving. It's just too bad they had to go.

I have admired Stompin' Tom Connors, a true Canadian who didn't want to move to the United States to make it big. Had Stompin' Tom wanted to go south and sing American songs I am convinced he would have been a huge star in the States. But he didn't want to go to Nashville. He wanted to be who he is – Canadian. Nothing wrong with that.

Smilin' Johnnie

He didn't want to sing Nashville songs. He wanted to do his own stuff singing about Canada and Canadians – the people and places he knew. I know you are going to tell me that Shania Twain does her own stuff. But she does not sing stories about Canadian places and Canadian things.

Can you imagine Stompin' Tom singing Syracuse Saturday Night? Probably it would have been a huge hit. But Sudbury Saturday Night, a Canadian classic, is not known south of the border. That's sad. But that's not what all this is about. That's just a part of it.

Radio stations over the years have played a bigger part in what we listen to than most realize – or will admit. Even the federal radio governing body Canadian Radio, Television and Telecommunications Commission has been bamboozled by the U.S. They have put in rules about radio stations having to play x-number of Canadian songs an hour.

What I don't understand is why don't they put a limit on the number of U.S. songs to be played in an hour, rather than the minimum number of Canadian songs.

I have come to believe that it is something in the Canadian psyche. We are too easy-going. Too forgiving. Too ready to fit ourselves into the slot where others want us to fit.

All this has made me a better person, not a bitter person. But I am getting ahead of myself. I have passion for this stuff. At least I have had passion for it over the years. I'll get back to some of this later on.

Now, let me take you back to my schooldays out in the parkland in those Dirty Thirties, when the economy was so poor and the world was focussed on the events in Europe, particularly in Germany. My Dad used to have me listen to Lorne Greene on the 9 o'clock news every night and tell him what was happening overseas. Of course, Dad was particularly interested because he knew the area that was then becoming a world hot spot.

2

THE DAY I BECAME 'SMILIN' JOHNNIE'

Every Friday afternoon we had a school concert. Every student was expected to participate. I am sure as I look back that it was meant to give us each confidence and self-esteem. There were 35 to 45 of us in the one-room school. We didn't have a stage. We stood at the front of the class and did our thing.

You could sing. Play an instrument. Dance. Take part in a play, recite a monologue, or a poem or read a chapter from a book. There was just one rule - you had to take part. There was no skipping this part of the school week. Everyone had to do something.

I was terribly shy and bashful.

This one particular Friday I remember well. I remember as if it were yesterday.

I always sang a song. It was always difficult for me to start singing, but when I once got going I liked it. This one day it was harder than usual for me to start singing.

Miss Kereliuk said "Okay, you, Smilin' Johnnie, hurry up. We have others besides you who want to do their part."

I was stunned. I was frozen.

The kids started laughing.

But all of a sudden the butterflies left me and I started singing. I got through

Smilin' Johnnie

the song and I thought that I would be able to rest – at least until the next Friday concert.

What I didn't expect was the ribbing I started to get from the children. They had picked up on the Smilin' Johnnie bit.

How little did Miss Kereliuk know that the name she called me would be the name that I would be known by for the rest of my life.

Perhaps more surprising to her would be the fact that I would be on stage. Singing. And professionally singing at that for more than 60 years. It would be my full-time work.

This bashful kid, who was too shy to sing in front of his class was soon singing to audiences all over Canada.

I have not made a lot of money being an entertainer, but I have made a pleasant, most enjoyable living for 60 years. Could I have made as much money over the years as a farmer? Probably. Would I have liked to be a farmer or a tradesman? Definitely not!

I am a poor man if material wealth and money in the bank are the only barometers of success on this earth. But I consider myself very rich, having lived a life I loved. I not only made me happy, but hope I have made others happy with my Smilin' Johnnie Show.

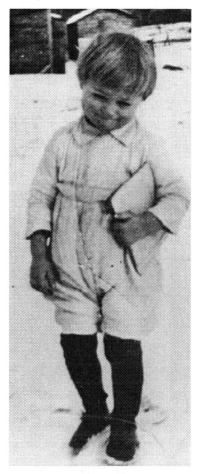

Johnnie aged 3 or 4 showing the kind of shyness that would eventually earn him his new name.

It would not be everybody's dream to go through life the way I am doing, but it was my dream, and I'm probably a little too stubborn for my own good, but that's not going to change now I am in my 80s.

3

GRANDMA LEFT 'NICE GOOD HOUSE'

My Dad, Michael Lucki, was born in Austria and came to Canada in the early 1900s when Saskatchewan was still the North West Territories.

He landed in Montreal from Hamburg, Germany, with his parents Stephen and Mary Lucki. In Austria they owned a little acreage with a house on it, but sold everything when someone told them "There is a free land. You can own all the land you want." That land, of course, was Canada.

Even with the wanderlust that is in me, I can't imagine what life was like back in Europe at the beginning of the 20th century when so many sold their entire life's possessions to buy passage on boats that today seemed all-too-small for that weeks-long trip across the Atlantic Ocean to a new and – hopefully – more prosperous life. Not necessarily better for them, but, they all believed, better for their children.

They gave up their comfort-zone of home. No matter how humble it may have been it was home. Family was there. Friends were there. Memories were there. And they stepped out in faith, to move half-way around the world, gambling on a better life.

They knew when they left home that it would be the last time they saw their parents, their brothers and sisters, their nephews and nieces, their grandparents. My grandfather had been working for the priest back in Austria. It wasn't that

Smilin' Johnnie

Johnnie was not much more than two-years-old out on the homestead with, from left, Grandad Stephen Lucki and Grandma Mary Lucki, Dad, Michael Lucki, Mom, Mary, Uncle Metro and Auntie Margaret.

The old homestead, built for Grandad by a contractor for $300 just before World War I.

Grandma left 'nice good house'

they were giving up a great life there. It was the feudal system and the Lucki family was neither among the lords nor the masters.

Mary was sick on the boat for three weeks and didn't feel better until she landed in Montreal.

She kept referring back to a "nice good house" she had left behind in Austria, until she came to Saskatchewan.

They didn't know anyone here. They didn't travel with anyone they knew. Just their little family on such a big and lonesome journey to a spacious land that they were eager to develop into a land the world would eventually envy. They didn't know the language. I know that thousands came to this country not knowing how to speak either English or French. And I am always amazed at how well – and how quickly – they fitted in to a new society and culture and master a new language.

They got to Winnipeg by train and settled where the Eaton's store was later built on Portage Avenue.

He didn't like it because there was no trees and no bushes. He wanted the whole bit – trees, land and all. The reason they wanted the trees and bush was because they wanted to be self-sufficient and the trees would have been their firewood and heat for the cooking stove.

When they left Winnipeg they only ran into more dissatisfaction. They moved to an area around Oakburn, Manitoba. The government dropped him off on the train line and there they had trees on their land, but there was no place to stay.

My folks made friends quickly with the local Indians. The native people loaned them spades and whatever else and they even helped my Grandad dig a hole in the ground in the side of a hill. Grandad cut trees and put poplar trees and sod on top for a roof and that was their house.

Grandad went out working and left Grandma with two kids. She told us that she used to cry when she heard the wolves and other animals howling at night. "I left such a nice home and they put me in the wilderness," she said.

I think if she had a chance she would have gone home in a heartbeat. But there was no choice. Travel wasn't as easy as it is today and credit wasn't as easy to come by. When the decision was made to leave Austria and come to the promised land of Canada it was a decision that was permanent. You had to make it work – or you were miserable. I don't think Grandma was miserable in Canada, but she had many sad days, especially early on.

Smilin' Johnnie

I remember them telling me about an incident when a priest came along to visit with them. He stayed overnight and it started to rain. In the morning when they got up there was nothing but mud. The mud was all over everything. And this was inside their 'house.' Of course, this was the sod roof leaking and partially collapsing.

They farmed the land at Oakburn, but they were not there very long. Grandad would go away for two weeks at a time to get a bag of flour and groceries – sugar, flour salt. The staples.

Grandma was right it seems. It was the wilderness – or at least they could probably see the wilderness from there. When you have to travel two weeks to the nearest 'grocery store' to stock up with staples you know that you are a few miles away from civilization – or the nearest rail line or road.

They were not happy with that place. Eventually they decided to move again. But you just didn't make a telephone call, get a mover to come in, pack and leave. You just decided which direction you wanted to move – north, south, east or west. Then you started walking.

He walked west. The west was in its infancy. Land was plentiful, but a lifetime of work came with every section. Trees and brush needed to be cleared. Houses had to be erected. Roads and driveways needed to be built. I don't know how these pioneers did it. But they did. And our lives today are so much more pleasant thanks to technology – and, of course, thanks to the pioneers themselves who struggled and laboured, often with the most primitive homemade tools to carve out a beautiful country from the virgin bush.

When he started walking from Oakburn, Grandad covered 125 miles before he saw some land near Wroxton, Saskatchewan. How long it took him, I don't know. How he crossed the mighty Assiniboine River, I don't know. I don't know how he managed on the trip. I guess so many people were pulling off these super-human feats – walking multi-marathon miles - to get a permanent footing on Canadian soil for their families that it probably wasn't regarded as a big deal back then.

You know, I don't remember ever talking to him about how he walked to Wroxton. It's only at times like this when you start to write a family history that you realise there are gaps in the story. And, of course, those who could give us the facts and tell us the story, have long since passed on.

I do know that Grandad was a big man. Six-foot plus and tough as nails. He bought land two miles north of Wroxton. They got their mail three or four miles away at Starlight, NWT.

Grandma left 'nice good house'

He was not satisfied with that quarter (160 acres) that had cost him $10.

So he moved again and bought a different quarter for $10 and that was to become the Lucki permanent residence.

When you bought land like this there was a promise involved that you had to clear the land as part of the deal. You had to 'prove up' your homestead.

They cleared it in instalments – five acres, then 10 acres, then 20 acres. They didn't clear it all. They left the wood for burning in the heater and the cook stove.

They grew wheat, oats and barley. It was all organic farming back then. There were no chemicals used. No fertilizer. No weed spray. They would go out into the field to pick out the noxious weeds.

They had sold their house and home back in Austria for fare to get to Canada.

Now in Wroxton, it was all beginning to look as though they did the right thing to move continents.

However, it wasn't all plain sailing. My Dad Mike had a younger brother, Metro. A terrible thing happened to him in a country school at Charkoff when he was 15.

A group of boys held him over a four-foot-wide well. They were threatening to drop him 30 feet into the water. They didn't, but just the sheer fright changed Metro's whole personality. He was never the same again. He was so terrified by the experience that probably didn't last much more than a few minutes, the effects stayed with him his lifetime.

Metro and Mike shared land. After the well incident my grandparents had them swap the land they owned because there was a better house on the land that was to be Metros, but Metro couldn't look after the grandparents.

Another sad story was when Grandad, who had bought another quarter section of land just south of the homestead, was burning stubble and the fire got away on him and was headed for his granary full of grain. He put out the fire, but he had what you would call today a heat-stroke. He lived just a few weeks and then he died. He was 75 or so.

Grandma was living with mom and dad. She was a good help around the garden. She loved gardening and in the fall she would gather kindling. She never liked to sit still. She had been a great partner with Grandad, but we never sat down with her and talked about life and her thoughts on some of the monumental decisions that were made by her and Grandad.

Smilin' Johnnie

Grandad Lucki donated land for this church two miles north of Wroxton. Grandad and Grandma are both buried there.

Relatives at Mom and Dad Lucki's 50th wedding anniversary in the early 1970s. Standing, back row, from left, Nettie Trafananko, Annie Bilyk, Sophia Kostiuk, Katie Slone, Johnny Mostoway, Dora Kostiuk and Maggie Galye. Front, from left, Mike Mostoway, Margaret (Lucki) Warcomika, Mary Lucki, Johnnie's Dad, Mike Lucki and Johnnie's Mom, Mary Lucki. The six ladies in the back row are Mom's sisters and Johnny Mostoway and Mike Mostoway are her brothers.

Grandma left 'nice good house'

One fall she got a cold that she could not shake. Dad took her to the hospital in Yorkton. She said: "Mike, I want to die at home." She died of pneumonia some days later. She didn't get back to the home that she loved so much and that she had sacrificed so much of her life to make it so very pleasant for those who lived there and those who visited. She passed away in hospital.

My mother's parents were Peter and Anne Mostoway and they had emigrated from the Ukraine. They had settled in the Calder area, about five miles from Wroxton.

Even though five miles was a long way in those days mom and dad met at a dance.

My mother went to Torsk School for two years, but she quit in Grade 2 when her Dad said she had better go to work. There wasn't the respect for education back then as there is today. It was more important to deal with the moment than prepare for the future.

She worked as a housekeeper and a cook for a Jewish businessman who was selling drygoods in Kamsack, probably about 20 miles from where the family lived. Her employer was good to deal with and was very hospitable.

Children didn't start school at five-years-old like they do now. I think Mom was 13 or 14 when she quit school in second grade and went to work.

I remember one incident Mom repeated to us when she saw girls walking around in bathing suits. She said that one weekend she came home from work to go to a dance.

She dressed up to go to the dance. She had bought a blouse with three-quarter-length sleeves but her Dad said she could not go to a dance dressed in the blouse. His thinking was "people will think I can't afford to buy you clothes. You are not going to the dance naked." And this was because of three-quarter-length sleeves! I can't imagine what his reaction would be if he had a chance to see a mini-skirt.

Grandad Mostoway got sick soon after drinking some home brew which was ice cold. He got a cold and lost his voice. He just couldn't talk. "If I can't talk to my grandchildren, I might as well die," he said. It was several months later when he died.

I was about five or six years-old at the time. I remember the neighbours built a coffin in his yard and a few weeks later I was building a little box. I said I was building a coffin for my uncle, Mike Mostoway.

Smilin' Johnnie

Johnnie and his Mom on the farm in Wroxton
when he was five.

Grandma left 'nice good house'

After Grandad died, Grandma, who had nine kids, went to live with each one in turn and when my parents opened a café, Grandma Anne worked as a dishwasher.

In the 1950s and 60s she spent some time in Toronto where some of the children had moved in the Depression Years to get jobs in the Campbell Soup factory. One started a service station.

My Mom and Dad lived on the farm until 1945, right after the war, when they moved to Wroxton and opened a café.

My brother Walter got married and moved to live on the homestead. But he only stayed a few years and then moved on and it became vacant. The land was rented out for a while, but no one lived there.

4

HAND-CRANKED GRAMOPHONE – 'A REAL TREASURE'

I was born in September 1924 about one mile east from where I live today. A lot has happened to me in the past 80 years. To try to keep it simple to follow I thought I'd better start at my beginning.

A midwife helped to bring me into the world. I don't think there was anything unusual about the birth and I don't remember much, if anything, about those early baby years. That's not unusual. I believe that the average adult can remember back to when he was three or four years old. Me, my earliest recollection is making the two miles trek from our farm to the school. In the summer, it was just good exercise for a young lad. You would have your farm chores to do before – and after - school.

You have to remember back then that children played a major part in the operation of the home. It wasn't like today, getting up in the morning at 8, having breakfast and going to school. Back then you would have your farm chores to do around the home. Almost as soon as you could stand there were things for you to do. And this was not make work

But in the cold, bleak winter, with the wind howling across the massive prairie and the snow blowing and drifting, Dad always hitched up the team to drive me to school.

We grew up quickly in those days. When I was 10 I was considered old enough to drive the team to school myself. This was no big deal back then. I wasn't the only kid who drove horses to school, especially during the winter months. Brandon was a one-room country school with 35 to 45 students from Grade 1 to Grade 11. One of the highlights of the year was the annual Christmas concert. And, of course, the weekly Friday afternoon talent shows in class obviously helped to prepare us for the Christmas concert.

Mother would sing as she went about her daily work and she would sing in the church choir – and in her later years, even at the jamborees we held at our property in the 1990s. I suppose this is what inspired my interest in music as a young boy - being exposed to it at school and at home. By the age of 10, music was all I could think of when I wasn't busy with school work or chores at home.

Another reason why school concerts were so popular was because there were presents for everyone. Our school had a unique way of choosing presents. We were told how much money we were allowed to spend (between 25 and 75 cents depending on the amount raised by raffle) and were asked to choose our gift from the mail order catalogue.

Most of the other kids would choose toys, pens, knives and such, but I would invariably order a mouthorgan, jew's harp, kazoo, or something to make music with.

When I was about 11 or 12, my Uncle Steve Bilyk loaned me his mandolin-banjo to plunk away on. During the winter months on the farm there were fewer chores to do, so the spare time I had was spent learning a few simple tunes.

Those winter evenings on the farm were really great. There was no television to occupy and waste one's time, and often not even a radio. Even if you did have a radio, the batteries would probably be dead. Batteries were 'expensive' and you didn't waste them listening to music. You had to make sure there was always enough power to listen to Lorne Greene read the news.

So there was nothing to do but learn music and create songs! Not too long after I had the use of the mandolin-banjo, I somehow managed to get hold of a most popular yet hard-to-get instrument, at least in our area at that time - a Palm Beach guitar.

If you had a Palm Beach you were a real musician! This particular guitar was tuned Hawaiian-style and I would spend hours singing and accompanying myself on the guitar, sliding the steel bar back and forth on the strings.

Dad was always great for attending auction sales. One day he came home

Smilin' Johnnie

from one of those sales with a real treasure – a hand-cranked gramophone and two 78s. This was the forerunner of the electric record player. When I look at what we have today with iPods - about the same size as a cigarette package - containing 5,000 songs, I really marvel at how much slower the pace was in those years just before the Second World War. But we didn't know any better.

Here we had a piece of machinery that was capable of playing music. Up to then we had to listen to the radio. Then we had to be satisfied with what the radio was playing. Now the gramophone was giving us a chance to play music we liked, when we wanted. The only catch was that you had to keep the gramophone wound up with a hand-crank on the side, similar to the handle used on a pencil sharpener.

The music quality was poor. Oh, it sounded alright as soon as you had cranked it up, but as it wound down it would distort the sound of the singer. As it slowed the singer had more of a croak until it stopped, often mid-song. Then there was no way to crank it up and continue with the record. If you did, the needle would jump and scratch the record.

And those records were made from a cheap, non-pliable plastic that cracked when you dropped it. They were easy to scratch. You only had to touch the gramophone - or the table it was on - and it would skip across the record and scratch it.

Some of the artists I used to like were Jimmie Rodgers, Carson Robinson, Gene Autry, and Rudy Vallee. We also had a couple of records by Wilf Carter, who was relatively new in the business then.

When I got that gramophone I spent all my spare time cranking it and listening, learning and copying the words to all the songs. From this wonderful machine, I managed to pick up some newer songs than the ones I'd known. Songs like *Frankie and Johnnie, Wreck of the Old '97, Red River Valley, Birmingham Jail, Back in the Saddle Again, Home Sweet Home on the Prairie* and many more. When my folks would listen to the records, they would say, "Johnnie, you learn to sing like those fellows on the records and maybe someday you'll have records of your own."

Of course, I scarcely needed any encouragement. I went right at it, spending all my spare time burning the midnight oil practicing. I would sing the songs over and over, trying to sound like the singer on the record.

Besides learning something, this interest in music always encouraged by my folks, also kept me out of mischief.

Hand-cranked gramophone - 'A real treasure'

One time my parents went to a party at the home of one of our relatives. Since this was before babysitters were heard of - kids got to go along to these parties. I really enjoyed this because it always meant music and I could get the chance to learn some more. At this party my uncles Johnny and Mike Mostoway played. Uncle Johnny played guitar and Uncle Mike the fiddle.

This was the very first time I'd ever seen two instruments played together. Just as I was memorizing the positions Uncle Johnny used on the guitar, he quit playing and started un-tuning the instrument, or at least that's the way it looked to me. I was sort of disappointed. But I kept on watching.

He took a piece of steel off the neck of the guitar and started tuning it again. When he began playing this time, he held the guitar differently and instead of using the bar on it, he was playing it with his fingers. Now my eyes really lit up. Now I really learned something different. It was then and there that I decided THIS was the way I wanted to play the guitar.

It wasn't until some time later that I realized what Uncle Johnny had done in that change. He had taken the steel nut from the neck of the guitar and changed it from a straight "A" tuning (Hawaiian) to Spanish-style tuning.

Needless to say, when we got home from that party, I didn't have enough spare time. My daily routine might have been something like this: 6:30 a.m. (or 7) my parents would wake me, 7:30 a.m. breakfast, 8 off to school. School started promptly at 9 a.m. and before classes we recited *The Lord's Prayer,* then sang our national anthem, *O Canada.* At noon we had our lunch, usually home-made jam or egg sandwiches. We ate outdoors, weather permitting. School was over at 4 p.m. and it took me about 45 minutes to walk home.

From 5 p.m. until 7, I would help with the chores, herd cattle to the corral, help milk the cows and help my mother churn the cream, then it was time for supper.

After supper I was usually free to sing and play the guitar until bedtime. Many times I devoted more time and energy to music than to either the school work or the farm chores!

While visiting my Uncle Johnny later, he must have noticed my interest in guitars, so he lent me his National Dobro model guitar. Boy, what a thrill! I played it for several months, even played it and sang at a local church picnic just for fun and picked up 75 cents in collections! That was pretty good pay considering the hired man we had on the farm only got $10 a month!

Smilin' Johnnie

All too soon, Uncle Johnny needed his guitar, so I had to return the prized possession and go back to my 'old' Palm Beach. Even this Palm Beach was borrowed, but it's owner, Peter Zipchyn landed a job with my folks on our farm, so I was sure happy!

Peter also played fiddle. After his farm work and my school work was done, we'd play for hours, tunes like *Alexander's Ragtime Band, Isle of Capri* and *I'm an Old Cowhand*. I believe we spent so much time playing that the only time the horses were fed or the cattle watered was when

Uncle Johnny, who loaned Johnnie a guitar and encouraged him to play music, with his wife, Winnie and two halloween revellers.

they could make enough noise to be heard over our music. I'm quite confident that my folks realized at this time that I would never make a farmer, my mind was always - and only - on music.

To digress a bit, when I was a youngster, my folks were more strict with me than were most of the parents in the community. However, our schoolteachers were also pretty strict (by today's standards). Once in a while, a little leeway was allowed, but we could never get away with what most youngsters today take for granted.

There were hard and fast rules which were obeyed - or else! You did not talk back to parents, teachers or any elders. My Dad often reminded me to keep my ears open and my mouth shut. With these words; "Young boys and girls

Hand-cranked gramophone - 'A real treasure'

Brandon country school where Smilin' Johnnie got his name. Two teachers in front of the truck are William Trafananko, left, and Fred Tetoff, the band leader who took Johnnie under his wing. The students crammed-in and standing in the back of the truck would travel for miles on the dirt roads to go to another school for a sports, academic or social event. This was about 40 years before seat belts became mandatory.

are still green! Still have their mother's milk around their mouth!" In his own unique way and by the tone of voice he used, I was firmly convinced Dad meant whatever he said and would stand by it. When, on occasion, I got brave and tried to bend the rules, I soon found out that he meant it alright!

Not only were parents strict, but so were teachers. I recall one teacher, Dora Kirstiuk, at the opening of the school term. She introduced herself and said, "Now class, I want you to remember one thing, I am your teacher and you are my students. You will remember at all times that a good student keeps his ears open and his mouth shut, simply because I'm here to teach and you're here to learn and you can't learn while you're talking, only when you are listening."

Somehow, whether at home or at school, this strict discipline was done in love and concern for the student, or sons and daughters. Concern for the development of our character and mind. In later years I found myself using these same words with my own children.

You may think country school was a drag, but we had many, many things to interest us, including nature hikes (actually nature was right close to us, but we still hiked into the immediate area to learn about plants and trees, etc), and sports-ball was played with great enthusiasm all summer.

5

I GET MY FIRST GUITAR

I was enjoying everyone calling me Smilin' Johnnie and the shyness that created that name for me was pretty much gone. I realized that if I wanted to make music and sing that I couldn't be shy. I can still have butterflies when I step up to sing, but I still step up to sing. In fact, I was now looking for places to sing.

In our area during the 1940s, amateur nights were popular. I took part in as many as I could. Sometimes I'd even win first, second or third prize, singing the songs I'd learned from the old gramophone. Finally one day, Dad brought home a battery-operated radio and I spent hours listening and learning new songs.

The local radio station CJGX in Yorkton was holding a big Wheat Pool amateur night, and I learned that all the contestants would be heard on the air.

My Dad wanted me to enter, but I still didn't have my own guitar, so Dad said he would buy me a guitar if I promised to sing for this amateur night. I didn't think twice. This was a no-brainer. So off we went to Yorkton to buy a guitar.

My very first guitar, boy, what a great feeling to be shopping for my very own guitar. However, Dad and I were looking for different things in a guitar. He was looking at price tags, while I was completely ignoring such minor detail and was looking for the prettiest one!

Finally, Dad picked out a guitar and said, "I'll buy you this one." Then, I

I get my first guitar

even surprised myself, for what must have been the first time in my life, I summoned up the courage to disagree. I said "No, I want this one. I don't like that one."

We talked back and forth for what seemed like ages. I was a bit scared, but by now I was a 'rebellious' teenager and very determined, so I played my ace. I said, "All right, you can buy me that one, but I won't sing on the amateur night."

When I think of it now, it sounds terrible. Keep in mind I had never before gone against what my father said. But this wasn't an everyday occurrence.

To my surprise, Dad gave in without a fight. Well, that was the one and only battle I ever won with my Dad.

Oh yes, the difference in price – the guitar my Dad chose was $4.95 and the one he bought me was $6.95. It sounds silly in this age of inflation to worry about a couple of dollars, but money was hard to come by in those days. I was pretty pleased with my very own guitar and more than willing to enter the amateur night. That's one wonderful thing about strict rules - when they are bent a little you are so thrilled and overjoyed that you appreciate the things you get even more!

I entered the CJGX amateur night, our master of ceremonies was Bob Priestly and the show was held from the York Theatre in Yorkton, which was full to capacity. I had never been in front of a microphone before nor had I conquered my fear of audiences, so you can well imagine how scared I was. Then came my time to sing. Shaking like a leaf, I sang *It Makes No Difference Now.* I didn't win a prize, but I didn't care. I was just happy to be a part of the event.

Just imagine, I was on radio. Me . . . singing on the radio! This was the talk of the neighborhood in our little area. By the way, the winners were Ed Ruhr and orchestra from Melville, Saskatchewan.

Young as I was, people seemed to sense my devotion to music and I met and talked with many folks who helped me later on. One time I met Art Mills who was the CJGX radio station engineer. The main studio was in Winnipeg and only the transmitter was located in Yorkton. I had heard a fellow by the name of Ramblin' Red Ross sing and when Mr. Mills asked me if I sang, I said I did. He suggested that I come back in the spring, when CJGX would have their studio in Yorkton completed, and ask for an audition.

Smilin' Johnnie

An 'audition?' I kept that word in my mind for 35 miles and when I got home, I headed straight for the dictionary to find out what this thing called 'audition' was. Need I say anymore? When the studio in Yorkton opened, I got a ride into the city, went into CJGX for an interview and audition! I was young and still going to school, 'green' was the word, but I did get a hearing alright. The announcer, Johnnie Hayden, knew my inexperience (which must have been obvious), but he was very kind and gave me some encouraging words and some tips to follow. I went home happy, but didn't proceed any further at that time, due to school work.

However, I did spend hours practicing, rehearsing, singing and inventing different chords on the guitar. I say 'inventing' because I had no one to show me the chords or how to form them so I had to invent my own formations by guess work and by listening to the radio and records.

My mother and I would sit up until two or three in the morning, copying and learning songs from the radio stations like WLS-Chicago, KITE-Kansas City, KFAB-Omaha and many others. We had only a sprinkling of stations in western Canada, but we listened to every one we could pick up, including Slim Wilson on CKCK-Regina, Alberta Slim on CFQC-Saskatoon and we never missed the Happy Gang on CBC from Toronto.

My parents were eager to take me places where I could sing or play guitar for folks and a 10 or 20 mile trip then was more exciting and thrilling than a 200 or 300 mile trip is now! I do remember that CJGX in Yorkton was holding an Empty Stocking Fund one year at the end of November. It was a sort of musical program with artists and musicians donating their talent and time to raise money for the needy. The listeners would pledge certain amounts of money to hear their favourite artist. I was glad to have a part in that worthy cause one year and brought in $85 in pledges. At these functions I learned more about how to present a song in front of a microphone and an audience. And I began to lose my shyness! Some of the people I met there helped me later on - Art Gellert, Ed Lawrence, George Gallagher, Jack Reich, all well known Yorkton artists in their own field.

At one Empty Stocking program I sang one of the popular songs of the day, *There's A Star Spangled Banner Waving Somewhere.*

Joined first dance band at age 15

Music teacher and dance band leader Fred Tetoff with accordion students Betty Surjik, Muriel Thies and Johnnie.

6

JOINED FIRST DANCE BAND AT AGE 15

When World War II broke out, I was still in school, Grade 10, I think. When the government began drafting fellows, many local musicians who had orchestras were called into the services, and the local dance orchestras became very scarce. While in my tenth year at school, my teacher, Fred Tetoff, played accordion and had a local dance orchestra. In school he organized 20 or 25 pupils in a band which included accordions, fiddles, mandolins, guitars, drums and pretty well every instrument.

Although you might expect that I played guitar in that band, I didn't. I took up accordion. My brother Walter played fiddle and sister Kay the guitar. We were taught how to read music and play first and second harmony. These music lessons Mr. Tetoff gave us were after the regular school class, most of the time, from 4:00 until 5:00 p.m., with no extra pay for his services. The only thing he did earn for this was the respect of the ratepayers. Mr. Tetoff was held in great esteem in our district.

We were proud to have a man of his calibre as our teacher. He was just a young man then, earning some $350 a year, which is probably one reason for him having a dance orchestra. Sometimes he even had to go to his parents for financial help.

The pay for a dance band at that time was $2.50 per night for three musicians!

Joined first dance band at age 15

One day after 4 p.m., as the class was dismissed, Mr. Tetoff asked me to "stay-in." He said he wanted to see me. I thought, "boy, what have I done now?"

After all the students had left for home, Mr. Tetoff came over and said, "Johnnie, I would like you to play guitar for my dance band."

I didn't know what to say at first. I thought he was joking. Here I had expected to be disciplined and he offered me a job!

He went on to say that his brothers, Paul, who played banjo and George, who played guitar, would not be able to carry on with the band and he wanted me to play rhythm guitar. Sure, I sang and chorded on the guitar around the district, but I'd never played rhythm guitar with another instrument, except in fun. Then when I realized I would have to play rhythm for accordion and saxophone, I just didn't think I could do it. After all, I was only 15 or 16 years old.

Johnnie usually had a guitar with him wherever he went.

Furthermore, one of the strict rules my parents set for me to obey was to be home at sunset. They would never hear of me playing for dances. Of course, I was willing, but I felt hopelessly inadequate. Mr. Tetoff agreed to talk to my parents, if I really wanted to play guitar for him. I quickly said that it wasn't a case of my not wanting to, and then and there, I became the third member of the Night Swingsters. Here I was, playing with a real orchestra (perhaps that would be better worded "trying to play"). I received my share of the pay which ranged from 50 cents to $1.25 depending on the distance we had to travel. The farthest we went was 25 miles.

It took me quite awhile to get over the shock of my parents allowing me to play for dances, but it was with the strictest understanding that I played music and did not at any time fool around. The Night Swingsters were composed of Mr. Tetoff on 120 bass accordion, Oscar Gellert on Eb saxophone and

42

myself on guitar (not much of a guitar either, but then I wasn't much of a musician).

I found it terribly difficult at first because I hadn't played rhythm for a dance before. It was hard just to keep up! Furthermore, the tunes that Mr. Tetoff and Mr. Gellert played were, for the most part, strange to me. Oh, I might have heard them once or twice but I had to learn to chord to *Five Foot Two, Marie Elena, Ramona, Blues In The Night* and such in keys like, F, Bb, Eb, Ab. It really kept me sweating and I soon found that I didn't know nearly as much as I thought I did.

Neither Mr. Tetoff nor Mr. Gellert mentioned my inexperience or lack of knowledge, though I know they must have winced a good many times. I had previously only played in A, C, D, G, E and these flats were completely new to me.

I had no idea where to find them or how to form them. One time, while experimenting with different chords, I made a formation on the fingerboard that eliminated open strings and came up with an E-flat chord, from there on I gained momentum! Much later I found out that for 75 cents I could have bought an instruction book that would show all the chords both open and closed rhythm chords.

But I learned them the hard way. It didn't do me any harm mind you, but it sure took a little longer. When I joined the Night Swingsters, Mr. Tetoff reminded me, that although we were playing for dances under the most informal conditions, he was still my teacher. These were his words, "When we play at a social or dance, you may call me Fred and be one of us, but when you're back in school on Monday morning, I'm still Mr. Tetoff to you." Though it was confusing at first, I understood his reasoning later on; it was only common sense to show respect for a teacher and things must be kept in the right perspective.

My first paycheck - if you can call it that - was about 50 or 75 cents. The whole group (three of us) was paid $2.25 to $3.00 and we played from 9 p.m. until 3 a.m. with a one hour break for lunch. There were no loud speakers, no public address system. The crowds would average between 50 and 150 people.

As time went on, Mr. Tetoff decided to raise our price by about 50 cents, making it $3.50 for the three of us - $1.00 each and 50 cents for gas and car expenses! Well, he had a local war on his hands, people would say, "Imagine $3.50 just to play a dance, just who do they think they are?" It was unbelievable how the

Joined first dance band at age 15

Winter and summer, Smilin' Johnnie was always pressed and dressed ready for a dance.

people reacted to a small price increase.

But, as World War II carried on, the orchestras became more scarce, so even with the higher prices we still had lots of jobs. Actually we had more dance dates than we could handle properly and the price kept rising, not only in dance band rates, but in everything. Soon $3.50 for the band for the night, had jumped to $35 ($10 each and $5 for the car). Then the war time price freeze came along and it more or less kept everything stable for awhile.

About this time my Dad took sick and I quit school to help with the farm work. But I still played dances. One time Mr. Tetoff booked off and we had a free weekend. He decided it was time that we went out and had some fun too, so he asked me to come along, perhaps we'd get a couple of girls . . . ? Well I said sure, but my folks would never approve of this. I guess Mr. Tetoff must have felt that he could trust me because he suggested a very devious thing. He said that I should bring my guitar along and my folks would think we were going to play a dance so they would let me go! Please understand that this is strictly out of character for Mr. Tetoff to suggest, but he must have felt that my parents were overly-strict in this matter, and that I was very trustworthy.

This worked fine mind you, but I revealed it to my folks later on, and they didn't mind - we all had a chuckle out of it! They, (Mom and Dad and Mr.Tetoff), were only concerned with my well-being.

During the war years we learned songs like, *Lily Marlene, Coming In On a Wing and a Prayer, There'll Always Be An England, Four Leaf Clover,* etc. But if I had any spare time I would still, for my own enjoyment, run over the old ones like *Little Green Valley* and *My Blue Ridge Mountain Home.* You can see where the influence in music came from.

Teaching and running a band soon became too much for Mr. Tetoff, so he asked me to take over the organizing duties of the Night Swingsters because he didn't want to jeopardize his position as school teacher by having too much on his hands.

By this time I had received a call to join the Army. I had been toying with the idea of joining the Air Force because they had a base in Yorkton. However, Dad was still sick and unable to look after the farm and since I was the oldest in our family, he received a temporary postponement for me. At this time, Dad made it clear that after the war was over and he was able to work, I would have to go back to school and complete my education. He said the farm was not important, he would sell it or rent it, or get my younger brother Walter to work it.

Many times I would hear these words, "John, go to school so you won't have to work as hard as we did." My Dad had a year of school in Grade 1 and my mother perhaps two years, which was their reason for placing a high value on education. They wanted us to have what they knew so dearly they had missed. But being a young fellow, school didn't seem all that important to me!

I did enroll in a radio correspondence course from a school in Montreal, but I never completed it. Let's face it, there was just too much farm work and too many dance dates. My days were spent working four to six horses in the

Joined first dance band at age 15

Dapper-looking Smilin' Johnnie

field until 6 or 7p.m., then I'd un-hitch the horses and Dad would take over and feed, water and un-harness them. I'd have to hurry and get cleaned up and changed in time to have a bite to eat before leaving with Mr. Tetoff to play for a dance.

He had a really good vehicle, a 1937 or '38 Plymouth, so we were high class. As I mentioned before, dances lasted until 3 a.m. or later, so I wouldn't get home till about 4:30 a.m., then I'd try to get a couple of hours sleep before going back to the field at 6:30 a.m. There were many times that I would come home and change into my work clothes and lie down fully dressed so I could sleep longer while waiting for Mom or Dad to call me.

My Dad must have realized that I was dead-tired many times, because, sick as he was, he would get up and feed the horses for me and let me sleep a little extra. But at 6:30 a.m. I went to work in the field walking all day behind the implements. It seems so strange to me today to hear people going on a 20-mile walk-a-thon and getting sore feet!

Speaking of walking, one time we had a dance booked for Stornoway, seven or eight miles from home and being harvest time, Mr. Tetoff couldn't make it, so I decided I would take my accordion and fill in for him. I carried the 50-pound brute and walked to Stornoway (it didn't have a light-weight case either, my Dad had made a good sturdy case for it!). Oscar Gellert and I played for the dance then he drove me home.

Later on, we managed to get a tractor for the farm work and it was ideal for me because then I could work whenever I wanted to and could sleep when I got home from the dance if it suited me, or go right to work if I felt like it.

7

MY OWN SHOW ON RADIO

The Free Press Weekly, the Western Producer and sometimes the Yorkton Enterprise, provided our shopping information, as well as news, comics, penpals and the odd new song words. One time, while looking through the want ads, I came across an ad, "new public address system for sale," from a firm in Winnipeg.

I had never heard too much about public address systems except that people at Fairs and Exhibitions were using them and I thought they were great, so I made up my mind to order it. The PA system cost me in the neighborhood of $100 and included a 15-watt chassis, one microphone and stand and one speaker with about 50-feet of cord. This was a six-volt outfit, and you should have seen the activity around our place for awhile. We were sure draining six-volt batteries. My Dad and I would set up the PA system close to our old gramophone, then my mother would play records on it - our neighbors would come over to see where this loud music was coming from. We had a lot of fun with it at first, but finally the novelty wore off.

This, of course, was the first PA system in our district and the news spread quickly. Many people came to our dances just to see how the PA system worked. Public reaction was mixed, but we did acquire more dates and farther from home.

One time we were booked for two solid weeks. A total of 13 playing dates. I was afraid this might be more than we could take because we were all working during the day, but I thought we'd try.

My own show on radio

With only three or four hours of sleep daily, after a week went by, I was tired, but still eager to carry on. The second week was harder, but I was too stubborn to show any sign of weakness. The thirteenth consecutive night we played for Mr. and Mrs. Jim Osmack's wedding in the Willowbrook area.

This was the straw that broke the camel's back.

We had Mr. Tetoff on accordion, Oscar Gellert on saxophone, Peter Mysko on fiddle and myself on guitar. We played for the afternoon reception and early evening reception and I was fine, but with all the food and a few short drinks, I could feel the strain. Still I wasn't about to give up, but about halfway through the dance, with the place full of people and no fresh air to keep me awake, it was more than my tired body could take. I could not finish those extra few hours.

The next thing I remembered, I was at Mr. Tetoff's place. One day later, he couldn't wake me up and I slept that night and all the next day in his car. That evening when I got home, still tired, I decided that something would have to go . . . the music or the farm. I would either have to quit playing so many dances or quit farming. It was a difficult decision to make.

I liked music but the farm was Dad's and he wasn't able to work it and was depending on me to do it, so I arrived at no definite decision.

When the war ended, Dad wanted me to go back to school, but I refused. I had been away from it too long and really had no interest in going back.

He then decided to rent the farm and get a business in Wroxton, so we moved to town and there we opened a cafe and pool room. It was my job to place orders to the wholesalers, be the cashier and maintain the front-end. My mother had the most strenuous job, she was the cook. And what a cook she was. Her family, the Mostoways, had a great ability to make a meal in 10 or 15 minutes whenever you arrived. I don't know how they did, but they could all do it.

Mom had the knack and the love for food preparation, so she was a natural in the family cafe. Mom at one time used to head up a team of women who would do all the cooking and catering for local weddings, that's how much they liked it and that's how good they were at it.

The Mostoways were hard-working, out-going, very sociable and likeable people. When they walked in a room they were noticed. Some of the Mostoway traits we see in our children. Eleanor spotted it at first, but now we both see it very clearly and so often.

Smilin' Johnnie

Bill C.   *Ken D.*   *George*   *Molly*   *Jack H.*   *Audrey*   *Norman*   *Arlene*   *Ken P.*   *Bill L.*

This was the CJGX staff when Smilin' Johnnie had his A.M. radio show in 1945-46

While Mom was using her talents in the kitchen at the cafe, Dad, still not completely well, looked after supplies to the kitchen, such as fresh meat and vegetables. My sister, Kay, was still going to school but she filled in as waitress whenever she was home and brother Walter looked after the pool room. We often had extra help because the business was good and too much for one family to handle. The wartime prices were still in effect and I thought they were a real good idea, but they soon disappeared.

Assuming the responsibility of the cafe management, I had gradually phased out many dance dates, so Mr. Tetoff and Mr. Gellert made other arrangements. I played the odd date with boys living closer to Wroxton, such as John and Bill Mysko. Later their brother Walter also joined in.

Though I didn't meddle in dances full-time now, I had all the up-to-date equipment and instruments of the day and of course, the PA system, so I had frequent offers which I had to refuse.

I had worked out a different system now, and I didn't give up my music nor jeopardize our business venture, I made the two work together. One time, while on a business trip to Yorkton, I visited the new CJGX studio and met many of the staff. The production manager was a small man but a real live wire, whose name was Bill Liska.

Talking to him I found a sincere person who was genuinely interested in local talent getting air exposure. So I quickly jumped on the band-wagon and landed myself a weekly western show every Saturday morning at 7:05 a.m.

My own show on radio

This was, of course, with my folks and Mr. Liska's approval. A radio show at that time of the day and week fitted right in with the cafe business and seemed to be satisfactory to CJGX. The idea was okayed by Ken Parton, the general manager of the station, and my western request show became a reality. Here was the opportunity I needed to gain experience and popularity.

My Saturday routine went something like this . . . I would leave Wroxton about 5 a.m. in a 1942 Chevrolet, drive 25 miles to Yorkton and get into the studio, pick up and sort the letters, arrange all the requests and greetings and type them for the announcer. My program was from 7:05 until 7:30 a.m. After that I'd generally drop in at the Corner House (all night cafe) for breakfast. They were always listening to CJGX so I had some fans there, and I usually liked to get to know my fans whenever I could. By 8:30 a.m. the wholesalers were open

Smilin' Johnnie's
100 RADIO FAVORITES 100
SOUVENIR SONG BOOK
Number 1

and I'd be there with my orders for the cafe and pool room. I had to work them systematically so that I picked up the ice cream last, just before leaving for home, because we had no hydro-electric power at Wroxton, therefore, no deep freeze and the ice cream at that time was packed in ice packs, a real luxury.

The first announcer I had with this Saturday morning show was Stan Obodiac, who went on to become the publicity manager of Maple Leaf Gardens in Toronto.

I must admit the first few radio shows I was shaky, never having had any previous radio experience. Stan would read the commercials and greetings

50

Smilin' Johnnie

while I looked on nervously from studio B waiting for the red light to come on. It didn't take me long though to get used to radio work and as time went by I made many changes and improvisations.

After several weeks on CJGX the fan mail increased, there were more and more requests and some even wanted pictures of me. Right from the very beginning of my career, my main interest was pleasing and satisfying my customers and giving them their money's worth. Sponsor Crescent Creamery paid for the pictures, so I dashed right out and had postcards made up with my photo on them and offered them on the radio show for 25 cents to cover the cost of printing and mailing them. It seemed to me that we added something to the show every week. Every time I dropped into Mr. Liska's office he had some brand new fantastic ideas, he was a tremendous man for the job of production manager. He always believed that we had a lot of music potential in the Yorkton area and that we should get these different groups and individuals to make use of their talents. With this in mind, he organized many programs featuring local talent.

It was Mr. Liska who gave me a little bit of philosophy I've never forgotten, he said, "Whatever you make up your mind to do, do it to the best of your ability," then he'd follow it up by asking me to learn more songs, especially those being requested by the listeners. Many times I would copy a song from the record at 6 a.m. in the studio and sing it on the program that morning because it was requested. I took great pride in pleasing the fans, it gave me a sense of satisfaction and accomplishment, regardless of the time and effort involved.

I would like to stress that this radio program was free time to me. No money changed hands. I guess the benefit was mutual - the station needed live talent and I wanted to be on radio.

In later years, musicians who were greedy for more decided that they should get paid for their broadcasts and thus it is now impossible to get this kind of a deal from any radio station. And besides, the union doesn't allow it!

However, it was a most satisfactory arrangement and I felt it was a very fair arrangement too.

I perpetuated this schedule for over a year. In the summer it was fun, but in the winter months there were, naturally, more problems. In the mid-40s the winters were long and cold. We did not have the facilities to winterize the cars back then that we do now. For example, a block heater was out of the question because there was no electricity . . . there was no 15-30 heavy duty motor oil . . . our

My own show on radio

so-called highways were just plain gravel roads . . . and snow plows were slow to clear the road in winter and in some cases local municipalities didn't have such vehicles.

When a storm broke out the telephone communications were bad. There was only one phone in Wroxton serving a community of 250 people. It was a toll station that meant it was a payphone. Imagine that. One payphone for 250 people.

There were times in the winter when I got up long before 5 a.m. to get started on a Saturday morning, especially if it was stormy and cold.

'Yours for a smile' is how Smilin' Johnnie has signed his autograph throughout his 60 years in show business. This picture was taken during his time at CJGX Radio in Yorkton in the mid-40s.

We always kept the car battery in the house to keep it warm, but many times, even though I had the car started, the road to Yorkton would be heavy going and I'd have to shovel my way through some of the drifts that were just too much for the car to break through.

I don't know which was worse, the winter drifts and cold or the spring with its mud. Those gravel roads weren't exactly a picnic to travel during the spring thaw either, but I always managed to make it to Yorkton on Saturdays and I was happy to do it, even if I had to shovel to get there. This was my life-long

Smilin' Johnnie

ambition realized and no amount of trouble could dampen my spirits.

All these things, the radio program, the cafe business, were new and wondrous experiences for me. After all I was still just a young lad of 20. I guess because I was young, I noticed and was interested in everything. For example, besides my extra work, I would take orders for tailor-made suits; I demonstrated and sold electric-light plants and ordered one for the café. Before hydro came to Wroxton we had 110-volt power, thanks to a generator that brightened our café and living quarters.

I still continued to learn new songs and wrote many songs of my own. I played guitar for many local groups to earn some extra pocket money and also to satisfy my dominating interest in music that prompted me to go to see every travelling group that came anywhere near Wroxton. There weren't too many of them at that time, but a few names that come to mind; Langenburg Oldtimers, Ramblin' Red Ross, Ted Preston and later Norm Auni. Wally Smith and Art Gellert weren't really travelling groups, but I heard them on the radio.

Then of course, there was the Air Force recruiting group that stuck in my mind from a few years previous. I had heard them in Yorkton at the Knights of Pythias Hall which was called the Cave. I also listened to CHAB, Moose Jaw and heard Bill Schultz regularly and others like Bill Smith and His Ranch Boys, Tex Moran, Ted Watermanuik and Mrs. Sid Freeman, Shuparski boys and Stan Habinski, who later led the Cowboy Kings. I'd heard Bill Dmitri, Stu Davis, Phil Temple, Walter Bud and His Blossoms, from Regina, Sleepy and Swede, a traveling duet, and the Alberta Cowgirls from Winnipeg.

When Danny Romaniuk and his group, the Swinging Strings, came to Wroxton to play a dance, I wasn't about to miss that deal. To my disappointment there were only a couple of dozen people and Danny and the group played only a short while. I was hoping to hear a full night, but I believe Danny was more disappointed than I was! I decided to go and talk to him and I asked him to come back. He said he would if he got $65 for his band. I drummed-up enough courage to say, "I'll take the offer," and a date was set for early in November.

"Sixty-five dollars, you fool," was all I heard for the next few weeks, from my friends, my folks and my relatives. It got so I was almost believing it myself! When I thought of the fact that the going price for a local group was $35 to $45 I began to think maybe I was getting taken for a ride, but I'd made a deal and I thought Danny and his group were well worth $65 and more. So I advertised this dance and took my chances. When the evening arrived I was quaking in my boots, but I tried not to let on. We opened the hall and I started selling tickets.

Perhaps many people just came to have a good laugh at me losing $65 - plus the cost of advertising, the hall rent, etc. However, what happened was a packed house. All the people enjoyed the music and had a good time and when the dance was over, I paid Danny his $65 and he was happy. I paid the hall rent of $15, plus the cost of help at the door and advertising expense and was left with $125. This was a happy and memorable occasion for me. I'd never dreamed of doing that well. I had been prepared for the worst.

However, while I had that much money all at one time, I wanted to buy something that I could remember the occasion by. I looked through all the wholesale catalogues and decided to order myself the best wrist-watch they had, 14 karat gold case, 14 karat gold hands, sapphire dial, etc. That $135 watch did yeoman service for me. I wore it every day for many years. It was into the jeweller's a few times to be cleaned and some other minor repairs. It kept great time until I lost it fighting a fire at the farm in 1977.

During World War 2 CJGX Radio in Yorkton held shows to raise funds to help Britain's war effort. Smilin' Johnnie took part as a amateur in some of these fund-raising shows, but he's not in this photo from the Yorkton Rotary Club's Bundles For Britain show.

8

Birth of the Prairie Pals

One day in June, 1946, as I was doing my morning radio show, I noticed a few boys watching me. It was very unusual, because not too many people came around the studio at 7 a.m. After the program was over, these boys introduced themselves to me. They were attending St. Joseph's College in Yorkton, and had organized a western band and called themselves the Sunset Five.

These boys wanted to go into the Yorkton and Dauphin area during the summer months and earn some money for their next school term. They required transportation and a PA system. They offered me $25 a day plus all expenses such as hotel, meals, etc. for the use of the PA system and the car.

After discussing this proposition with my folks, they were quite certain they could manage the business for a couple of months during the summer with my brother Walter and sister Kay to help. After all, I would still be around on Saturday morning and could help my folks for the weekend.

The Sunset Five consisted of Wally Kowalyk, general spokesman, so it seemed, and fiddler, Victor Pasowisty, second fiddle, Ray Lazar played saxophone and clarinet. He was a more aggressive type of person, but a nice fellow as far as I could see. I believe the accordion player was Mike Chorney and Nick Dneterko played banjo. We got everything organized for the first date in Dauphin, but when we arrived no one seemed to know anything about it. There were no posters up. Each member blamed the other for not doing things right.

Birth of the Prairie Pals

Smilin' Johnnie, right, with his original Prairie Pals, from left, Victor Pasowisty, Alf Shingoose, Joe Regus and Ray Lazar.

There was friction with them on the first night. However, this didn't worry me. My job was to get them there on time. But the second night was the same, as were the third and fourth and on and on.

The deal was very shaky. I didn't receive payment for the nights they didn't get any money and they had no money to speak of in the first place. After all they'd organized the band to make money. However, being the only one with cash, I was having to finance the group's trips from day to day.

I suppose I didn't have to play banker, but I just couldn't leave these ambitious young fellows who were filled with enthusiasm and let them beg, borrow and steal their way home. Probably this was one of the reasons I never did get rich!

The boys kept promising reimbursement as soon as a jackpot crowd came along. By this time we ended up in a small place south of Dauphin, Mountain Road, which happened to be Victor's home town area. The boys had played a few dances in that area and done well financially, but I noticed they still had no system, nor any pattern to their bookings, the music on stage, nor the financial end of things. It seemed to me that each one in that group was there to see how

56

much he could get out of it and not what he could put into it. If any of them did accidentally manage to do the other person a good turn, they made sure everyone knew about it.

By now I'd been paid some money and some back pay too. I'd also learned that a bag of salted peanuts and a coke were good, cheap substitute for a meal.

I knew this group couldn't last long, but it was not up to me to say. Then one night, in the Ituna district, Victor and Ray quit the group. I could see that coming and I was ready to go home anyway.

Victor and Ray asked me if they could catch a ride back to Yorkton, so we left the others behind and

One of the original Prairie Pals, Victor Pasowisty, with Eleanor and Smilin' Johnnie at one of the 'Friendly Reunion' Jamborees at the Lucky family home.

were on our way back home. I very casually asked the boys why they were quitting just when things had started to pick up, they grinned sheepishly at each other and said, "Who's quitting, we just decided to join you and you could be our boss." Knowing how full of mischief these young fellows were, I thought they were just joking.

However, they soon made it clear that they really meant it. At first I didn't want anything to do with this deal. But they were determined to quit college, form a group and hit the road with me as their full-time leader. It was then that I remembered that several times Victor and Ray had hinted about me taking over the group, but it never entered my head that they were serious. They were serious alright, no matter what excuse I had, they had the answer. I had been a leader of a local group for a short time and I didn't feel competent to lead a group commercially, but the boys assured me they'd help with all the problems. I said I'd have to be at Wroxton weekly to help with the family business. They said they would even wash dishes and carry wood and water if need be.

So here I was, without even trying, the leader of a commercial group. Well, not quite. We had a fiddle, saxophone-clarinet and guitar, but needed an accordion player. This was a must at that time. You never had a band back then without an accordion player.

Instead of going back to Yorkton that evening we headed for Regina to look for an accordion player. Here I was, just nicely getting started to pick up a few ideas musically, when I was placed in the harness of the boss. I didn't really know what I was doing, yet I was responsible for hiring, firing and sifting through musicians. We drove through Regina and Moose Jaw, made calls, and listened to a dozen or so accordion players, but none were satisfactory. Either they wanted too much money or they just weren't what we wanted or they didn't want to go on the road.

Many who would go on the road didn't even know how to hold an accordion properly. We got a tip one day though and this took us to a small town north of Weyburn, a place called Cedoux. Here was an accordion player. Vicky Jenesco played the 48-bass accordion. Nothing fancy, but clean cut. More important, she was a well-mannered girl and was interested in road work. We were hoping to get a man who played 120-bass accordion, but after all the searching we decided to accept Vicky. Besides she had previous road experience which was helpful, so she was hired.

We all spent a lot of time organizing the group for the road, but the biggest strain was on me, even though Victor and Ray promised to help they seemed quite satisfied with the way I was handling the band. I guess they'd learned that in order to get out of extra work, you refrain from complaining about the way others are doing their job.

They left it up to me to get the radio program, make the posters, book the halls, send out the advertising, get uniforms, decide which songs and tunes to play, look after the transportation, accommodations and also look after the cafe business in Wroxton.

There was also the Saturday morning radio show. And we still needed a name for the group. Some of those people who think this business is a real soft touch ought to try it sometime.

Smilin' Johnnie

Knowing Bill Liska, we had no problem getting on the radio twice a week on the Farmer's Hour program. Mr. Liska would have liked to give us more time, but the general manager, Ken Parton, had already okayed two or three days for a group called the Cowboy Kings who had been working out of Regina and Moose Jaw and had quite a bit more road experience than we did. Vicky knew this group and told us they were "tops" and that we'd have some pretty stiff competition from them. They were all seasoned musicians, not green-horns like us. I braced myself for the worst with my young, enthusiastic group and figured if worst came to worst, I still had my Saturday morning show and I knew that I had a lot of listeners at that time who didn't or weren't able to listen later on during the day. So I used my morning show to let my listeners know that we had a dance orchestra available for bookings in the Yorkton area.

I used to get mail from Saskatoon, clear through to Winnipeg and from North Dakota to Nipawin, even though Yorkton was only a 1,000-watt station at the time.

All the patients at Brandon T.B. Sanitarium had breakfast to my Saturday morning show. Before long, I had a sponsor for the morning show. Crescent Creamery in Yorkton agreed to send a free picture of me to anyone who shipped · a five-gallon can of cream to them and in return I would announce our dance dates on the morning show.

By this time, many of my listeners wanted me to pay a visit to their town, so the bookings were coming in and our little group of amateurs was on its way!

Victor, Ray and Vicky did a lot of work on the music end of the business and also came up with ideas for bandstands and uniforms. This left me a little more time to make bookings for the group and get posters printed. Still nobody had thought of a name for our group. besides "Smilin' Johnnie" and with a girl in the group it ruled out using, "Kings or boys, etc.," so our choice was limited. One day while in the Balmoral Hotel in Yorkton with some announcers from CJGX, Bill Clark and Jack Goodman, we asked them for advice. They both agreed that we needed a simple name and an original one, but it was Jack Goodman who suggested "Prairie Pals" and that's the name we chose in 1946.

9

AMATEUR NIGHT IN WROXTON

I found out quickly that being the boss was just a glorified title for a work horse. It meant being up before everyone else (remember, even on the farm I wasn't an early riser!).

It meant planning your day, your week, your month and carrying out these plans. With bookings, I'd have to spend about two to four hours daily in the phone booth making arrangements, the telephones were still not efficient. In other words, it meant that I had to eat, sleep, drive and think music 24 hours every day. Just one slip and "Well, you should have known better" was the word from members of my group.

Our first dates in the Yorkton area were within a 50-75 mile radius, but with the pressure of the now-established Cowboy Kings, our dates gradually extended farther and farther to avoid too much competition. But, never-the-less the competition grew keener. If one group had two-color posters, it was certain that within days the other group would try to out-do them with an added feature. Besides the Cowboy Kings, we had many local non-professional groups sprinkled all over the Yorkton area, all scrambling to get publicity on CJGX for themselves.

There were also many new announcers coming into CJGX. I have forgotten many, but one that sticks in my mind, who was a pillar at CJGX was Molly George. I listened to her often. She also played a real good trombone in the band which her father directed.

Smilin' Johnnie

Mr. English and Jack Shortreed were at the station then, of course, and I also remember a few of the younger boys just beginning to break into announcing; Norm Runtz, Jack Henderson, George Gallagher and Ed Lawrence. We watched these fellows go through their learning period at CJGX.

We saw more and more small groups starting up and eventually we would see them at the radio station. We met many musicians this way. Although Vicky had quit, we were doing well and by winter we decided to expand to stay competitive, so we added Alf Shingoose, formerly of the Langenburg Oldtimers, on accordion, piano and banjo, and Joe Regus from Fenwood on drums.

We were now a five-piece group, working hard arranging and re-arranging tunes, trying to improve our dances and radio shows. Everyone pitched in and did their share. We met other musicians too; Norm Auni, Ted Preston, Danny Romaniuk (whom I knew previously), Gary Scholz, Chuck Dixon, the Berting Boys, Johnnie Manz, Bill Smith and the J B Ranch Boys, plus a host of others. This might come as a shock to those who think we didn't have much Canadian talent, but these people were real top musicians and still there were more bands creeping into the CJGX area and working out of Yorkton.

Our dance dates carried us as far as Neepawa, Manitoba and Watrous, Saskatchewan and from Prince Albert to Estevan area. Still we were taking in other towns closer to Yorkton as well.

Needless to say, when we got rolling, we played steady. I remember one time we started in April and played seven nights a week straight through until the end of October, as well as doing our radio shows. We were drawing anywhere from 100 to 400 people per engagement, the admission was 75 cents and hall rates were anywhere from $5 to $20 or a rare 75-25 per cent split with our share being 75 per cent. Hotel rooms cost 75 cents to $1.75 each, posters were $35 to $75 for 3,000 (18-inch x 24-inch two color) and postage for posters was one cent each, letters were three cents.

If our attendance dropped below 75, we shut it down at midnight and gave them their money back. We needed the rest. We were all young, but slugging seven days a week was still tiring.

Still everybody had lots of energy and kept coming up with new ideas for music or posters or something. I guess, looking at us from the sidelines, others must have thought this was the ideal get-rich-quick scheme, so more and more groups came in to Yorkton to jump on the 'band' wagon. Like I said,

Amateur Night in Wroxton

our youth carried us along with enthusiasm, but it was still a tough grind and nerves were pretty well frayed after a few weeks.

Though we had a good group and the crowds kept coming, the large following was probably due to the solid support we got from Bill Liska's production manager's office at CJGX. But when it came around to the month of March our crowds dropped off drastically. Almost no one attended because of the lenten season which was observed by many of our fans in the Yorkton area.

Lent would automatically cripple our business for five or six weeks. For young, ambitious, enthusiastic fellows this was just too long to be idle, so one year I got a brain wave! I suggested to Victor and Ray that we hold an amateur night in Wroxton similar to the A.C.T. shows, a sort of forerunner of America Idol or Canadian Idol.

We decided we'd do it all on our own and hold it right dead centre in the Lenten season. They both agreed this was a great idea.

So we rented the hall and got our posters printed at the Redeemer's (Catholic) Press in Yorkton, which brought another idea to mind . . . why not give 10 per cent of the net gate receipts to the Catholic churches in Yorkton and get one of the priests to come and give a little speech for the amateur show?

We weren't really con men, just young fellows experimenting with whatever ideas came to mind. Thinking we would try to get as many 'big' names as we could, we got Mr. Liska to come and emcee the show. We also hired Alf Shingoose, Jack Reich and a couple of other musicians to play intermittent music. To bring these people from Yorkton, we had to hire two or three cabs. Victor and Ray looked after selling tickets at the door for the evening, but we had to have help later on when Victor and Ray went around the audience collecting votes.

You see, we'd got the idea of the audience buying votes for their favourite contestant from the practice at A.C.T. amateur shows. So we sold the votes for 10 cents each and the contestant who brought in the most votes got the prize. I remember my Mom and Dad relating an incident to me later . . . Victor and Ray were selling votes, when Victor called to Ray, "Ha, ha, I've got $5 worth of votes on so and so!," and Ray happened to be standing beside an opposing contestant's father, so Ray said, "Are you going to let him get away with that?" That brought in $10 worth of votes from the father who wanted his daughter to win. The way it took place and the way my folks related it, they had tears of laughter.

Smilin' Johnnie

Engineer Art Mills, seated in the middle of the front row, with CJGX staff in 1946.

Like I said, Victor and Ray (and myself) were young and full of mischief. We still had access to the radio waves, so we plugged our amateur show every chance we got and really talked it up.

What began all in fun turned out to be wall-to-wall people at the hall in Wroxton on the evening of the amateur show. After the show Victor and Ray had a tub full of money they took back to the cafe to count. Perhaps anyone who would have seen us would have been pretty envious and jealous, but the people did have a very enjoyable evening and we had incurred a lot of expense for publicity, music, emcee, etc., so it was a benefit to the community. We grossed $750 that night and after paying all our expenses, Victor, Ray and I were left with about $400 clear for our work.

What had started out as a harmless joke had paid us well, even though we'd really put a lot of work into it and this would have to keep us through the rest of the lenten season.

10

MANY JUMPING ON 'BAND' WAGON!

Looking back on those early days of the Prairie Pals it is almost unbelievable just how much competition there was between the Yorkton groups.

They pulled tricks and stunts on me and my boys to get our group – and other groups – disorganized. They might get someone in your band drunk, which would put the person out of commission for just a day, maybe two. And if they did it during a dance that could be very disruptive and even cause the band to have to quit performing for the night – or maybe even longer.

And once the group was thrown off by comments or tricks from a competitor it took awhile to get things back on track.

These competitive bands picked on a musician and then played on his weakness. The most common weakness of a musician was drinking. When a musician was drunk that would naturally throw a monkey wrench in that band's music for the evening.

When in Yorkton, it seemed, the meeting place would usually be the local beer parlour, side men with side men and bosses with bosses. We'd talk shop, gossip and try to keep a straight face while undermining the opposition's business. We were a young group, Alf Shingoose was the oldest, a treaty Indian, a very versatile musician and a likeable fellow, easy to get along with, he was our key man. The other bands knew this and whenever the opportunity would arise, they would ask Alf politely to come for a drink, but they never stopped with a sociable, drink. They knew full well that Alf couldn't handle too many drinks and was too easy-going to refuse them, so they'd pour a dozen drinks into him knowing exactly what effect this would have on our band.

These things always seemed to happen just before our radio show. However, we did the best we could with what we had. Sometimes we had to use a substitute.

Financially we were doing well, perhaps too well for a bunch of young guys with lots of energy. With all our prosperity we bought new instruments, new clothes, disc recorders, radios, (for every radio at that time, you had to have a license which cost $4), more instruments and a new car. Cars were pretty hard to come by at that time. There was a long waiting list when you ordered a car. But if you ordered an expensive model the garage would put your name up nearer the top, so I ordered a Deluxe Chevrolet, a bigger car than the average farmer would buy and I ordered it complete with all the available accessories at that time.

The most noticeable extra probably was 'Smilin' Johnnie and His Prairie Pals' written along the sides of the car in 14 kt gold leaf lettering. Then of course, we had a rack on the top for the instruments. The total cost of the car, complete with accessories and lettering, $1,850. However, money was coming our way and we invested it to improve our service. Perhaps the peak years of our musical career in Yorkton were 1947 and 1948. Despite the problems and difficulties we encountered we were going ahead at full steam.

By the spring of 1948 there were at least 18 bands working out of Yorkton and most of them were given some radio time to get publicity. Therefore, we didn't dare let any grass grow under our feet or we'd have been left way behind. We didn't dare miss any radio broadcasts either, so I made arrangements to record some shows on transcription discs which were the size of 12-inch LP discs or a large pizza, just in case any member happened to get led astray by the competition and not be able to play for the broadcast. Tape recorders hadn't been invented yet or hadn't become popular in our area.

With the good revenue and heavy workload, came the musician's Number-One enemy of that time, booze, liquor - whatever you like to call it. Later, the enemy was drugs. But no matter what form it takes, it seems the entertainment business is prone to damage from this enemy. I certainly could notice it invade our little group. It began very subtly with Alf Shingoose not being able to control his liquor. Usually Alf had to be led on, but the other boys didn't need any encouragement, they got drunk on their own.

Many jumping on 'band' wagon

I don't mean to say that the group immediately became a bunch of drunks, but first it was one too many drinks at a wedding dance, then it was a bottle for some occasion until it became common place for one or the other to be under the influence of liquor.

I'm not saying that I didn't join in, I drank right along with the boys. At first I just wanted to be sociable. Later on I drank to keep them from getting too much. I tried to make them see then what liquor was doing to our close-knit little group, but nobody would listen to me, much less quit drinking.

One day I walked into the studio just before our show and noticed a tramp standing there with torn pants, worn out shirt, sloppy torn shoes, unshaven. What a sight. He smiled at me and introduced himself, "I'm Tex Moran." I stood there dumbfounded. I knew who he was all right, not that I'd seen him before, but I'd sure heard about him. Tex Moran was the best. A top fiddle, guitar, banjo and bass player. But I just couldn't believe this tramp was him. However, when Alf Shingoose came in, he assured me that it was Tex. Tex was flat broke and didn't even have a fiddle string to his name, much less a fiddle. After listening to his hard luck story, I took him in . . . an hour later he played with us on the air.

The telephone wasn't as popular then as it is now, and only occasionally did anyone call the station after the program. But after Tex played, there were many, many calls complimenting us on the music. So I thought anyone who could create that much interest in such a short time was well worth keeping.

After the program we got Tex some new clothes, uniforms, shoes and, of course. a fiddle.

I had visions of the boys buckling down now and perfecting more tunes and forgetting about the bottle. What I didn't realize at that time was that Tex had more of a drinking problem than all of our group put together. He went from bad to worse. Not only did Tex drink beer and wine, but also vanilla and lemon extracts. On some of our repeat jobs, long after he was gone, the local storekeepers would present me with a bill for a dozen or so bottles of extracts charged up by Tex Moran in my name.

After three or four weeks of this, it was my sad duty for the first time, to fire a man, one of the finest musicians and entertainers we'd ever heard. By firing Tex on the spot, I thought I'd kill two birds with one stone, I'd get rid of a bad influence on the boys and possibly they'd take heed and snap back to attention. Somehow I failed, because it wasn't long before I had to use the same treatment on Alf Shingoose. We used Ray Lazar's brother Wally on

Smilin' Johnnie

Smilin' Johnnie with one of the best musicians he ever played with, Tex Moran. Unfortunately, Tex had a drinking problem.

accordion. He was only 17 but a real good little accordion player and very set in his ways for a young lad.

We built up many regular dates in our area, such as Gorlitz, operated by Mr. and Mrs. Jim Filipchuk; Fork River, Manitoba, operated by Nick Panko at that time; Riverside Hall operated by George Ricker; and Redvers, Saskatchewan. operated by Mr. MacDonald Other towns I've forgotten the hall manager's name - Wadena, Sask., Virden, Manitoba, Fishing Lake Pavilion (Pop Paulson and his wife operated this until the late 60s), Daphne, Crystal Lake, Kenosee Lake, St. Gregor (we used to get 300 or more people every second Monday), Clair, Goodeve, Benson, Greenwater Lake, the Arcade in Prince Albert, the Arcade in Neepawa, Manitoba, the Trianon, Regina, Danceland, Watrous, Temple Gardens, Moose Jaw, Mitch's Barn, north of Brandon, Manitoba and the Brandon Palladium, operated by Albert Johnson, who had a great band himself in the Brandon area.

The Old Foxford Hall, in the Weirdale area north of Prince Albert, brought

Many jumping on 'band' wagon

us a surprise. We rented the country hall for $10, but it didn't have hydro, or lights. We had over 700 people on a Saturday night and played until 4:30 a.m. when the sun came up. That's the kind of reception we were getting once the name was built up. Because the money was good, there was lots of opposition, everybody wanted to cash in on what they thought was this easy-money game. We not only had opposition in the Yorkton area, but also the local bands in every area.

Prince Albert had Uncle Jim and the Oldtimers, from Saskatoon there was Ernie Howard and the Farmer Fiddlers, The Primrose Ranch Gang, Frank Callaghan, Ken Peaker and his orchestra; from Regina and Moose Jaw there were scores of groups including, Bob Giles, Dick Lilico, Ernie Lindell (then going under Smilin' Ernie), JB Ranch Boys, Happy Russell, Slim Wilson, Alberta Slim, Bill Dmitri, Stu Davis and a host of others.

Out of Winnipeg we had; Glen Frain and his Buckaroos, Fred Haddaler, Frank Staff, Andy Dejarlis, Pat Pender, Nick Wally, Patterson Playboys' and many more.

Then there were the bands working out of Yorkton - The Cowboy Kings, Paul Perry and Orchestra, Gene Dloughy all were gaining momentum. Each of these had their separate areas, but naturally we overlapped and ran into each other sometimes. There was money being made and everyone wanted his share.

While we musicians and bandleaders were making a pretty nice buck, our co-buddies, the announcers who emceed our radio shows were not doing too well financially. Many times their bacon and eggs were on us, especially the younger ones.

I well remember being in Bill Liska's office when one of the young announcers complained to him about low wages. Mr. Liska said, "You choose the career you liked best, next comes sacrifice, then comes learning the job and then comes, don't complain - if you're looking for big and quick money, then take a job in a mine or a lumber camp or construction."

Mr. Liska went on to say, "You must sacrifice certain things in life if you want certain things from life." He added that even his wages were too small and far below what he needed to keep his wife and family, but one must choose.

They both got their wishes for a bigger paycheque. That young announcer went on to become a part-owner of CJGX radio station and Mr. Liska became production manager at CBC in Winnipeg.

11

Honeymoon in Nashville

In November 1948 I got married to Sylvia Klym, from Sandy Lake, Manitoba, a young lady I met at one of the dances I played. People who were in radio and the music business had been telling me I should take my group to Nashville and the Grand Ole Opry, so I thought I would combine business with my honeymoon.

Instead of taking the whole group, my wife and I went down to Nashville to see just what was going on there. We spent some time in Nashville, going to the Grand Ole Opry and meeting some of the performers, but it certainly didn't take long for me to find out that what I thought was competition back in Yorkton, wasn't anything compared to what went on in Nashville. The pace was double what ours was back home and I could see that it was a cut-throat business.

People smiled, but not to be friendly. It was only a formality. They were actually ready to pull the rug out from under you. Everyone seemed to be elbowing their way in so they could be "first."

It sure didn't take me long to make up my mind that this was no life for me. Going full throttle most of the day and most of the night, my nerves wouldn't take it. I'd have to weaken and resort to booze or pills or something like many of the entertainers there did in order to keep up. I liked music very much, but I couldn't see myself sold out to it.

Honeymoon in Nashville

Sure I was dedicated to my career, but I wasn't fanatical about it. I did meet many fine folks there at that time and I remember a few; Fred Rose, Roy Acuff, Eddie Arnold, Ernest Tubb, George Morgan, Little Jimmie Dickens and Cowboy Copas.

I went to a number of music houses, publishing houses and during the course of conversation, I learned a lot about how the many groups survive the many intricacies of this music business. Some were good, some were bad. But all were slanted and employed to make the bucks more rapidly regardless of the consequences.

This trip to Nashville, at this time, answered, in living color, many of the questions that had been in my mind for a long time.

I came back to Yorkton satisfied that it is better to be a big fish in a little pond than to be a little fish in an ocean, especially since our little pond was still relatively free of pollution.

Returning from Nashville, we tuned our instruments, pressed our uniforms, greased the car and were back on the road, playing job after job as before, only this time exchanging with the boys in my group some better ideas I had picked up across in the U.S.A.

After a short break everyone was eager to work and for a while it was like old times. But this only lasted a short while, then once again I noticed frequent visits to the liquor store, which became so obvious that even some people at the radio station noticed.

Something I learned in Nashville was that I should have listened to Mr. Liska and made recordings as soon as I landed a radio show on CJGX. Even though it was a little late, I wrote all the record labels we had in Canada (and those were very, very few) asking about the chances of making a record with them. But to my surprise I wasn't even able to get to first base.

I personally didn't like my voice on record, but as a band we put out some pretty good stuff and I was disappointed that none of these companies were even remotely interested and they came up with the queerest excuses when they replied, everything was 'don't call us, we'll call you.'

This did not help to keep the boys interested and working, it just called for another drink.

I didn't quit enquiring about the recording business and it always seemed to end up the same way, no matter who I asked, from the radio station people

Smilin' Johnnie

to the members of parliament, it was always the same answer - you have to become popular first, then the recording company's 'scouts' pick you up, put you on records and you're away, only they used the fancy word 'discovered.'

However, by this time, I told these people we'd played all of Saskatchewan and Manitoba from end to end, side to side. Surely in three years we would have run into one of those 'scouts' - at least to have a talk to. If these 'scouts' can't discover us, in three years, maybe we could discover the 'scouts' some place!

Smilin' Johnnie's first wife, Sylvia, in the middle, with Steve Warcomika and Jean Bryski, a neighbour.

Well, it was all a farce. We never did see any of these 'scouts,' and neither did the four or five dozen other top groups that we knew then. It was just an empty excuse pawned off on local musicians. We didn't matter. We weren't legitimate business.

This was the beginning of my realization that even our members of parliament and legislature were uninformed and couldn't give us an honest answer. I thought, if these people didn't know about something they were asked about, they should find out and not just pass it off as quickly as they could. We just wanted to get on records because our fans had requested records, but how to get on records?

As our popularity increased, regardless of the irritating drinking problem,

Honeymoon in Nashville

we received requests from many distant places in Alberta, Ontario and also in North Dakota and Montana. These Americans wanted our 'Canadian music' - I didn't even realize there was such a thing.

When we inquired about taking bookings in the United States however, we found that we could not go across the line. Oh, we could, technically speaking, but the red tape involved was a mile long and might take the U.S. government four to six months to okay it. The U.S. government's main reason for not allowing Canadians across was simply that we would be infringing on the employment rights of the U.S. musicians. At first I thought this was some kind

A promo shot of Smilin' Johnnie, with a Frank Gaye guitar. They were made in Edmonton and were used by several Opry stars, including Ray Price, and Webb Pierce.

of a joke, but I found out later that it was a strict law enforced at the customs house and even if you were okayed you had to be bonded.

Now this is as it should be. I have no argument with the U.S. law at all, only why didn't Canada have the same kind of law? Simply, Canadian musicians could not play in the U.S. without a lot of rigmarole, but American musicians could perform in Canada no questions asked.

12

Politicians don't understand the business of entertainment

If there is a disappointment in my 60 years in the entertainment field it is that I have not been able to get the Canadian governments interested in recognizing entertainment as a legitimate industry in our country.

I still believe that if the federal and provincial governments would make it as difficult, or inconvenient for Americans to work in Canada as the U.S. authorities make it for Canadians to work in the U.S., more Canadians would be able to make a living on stage.

We are not talking brain surgery here. But it would take politicians who are not afraid to stand up to the Americans. I don't know what it is, because the things I read don't show that we have a good relationship with the Americans. I don't know what we stand to lose politically if we start battling the Americans. Then, when I see how the Americans thumb their noses at us over softwood lumber, I can't help but think that all the fuss and talk over free trade between the U.S. and Canada back in the Mulroney years has not been understood in the same way by the two countries. Or is it just a case of political bullying?

We seem to be scared of their shadow. We don't want to take them on. I have no reason why.

I began to write to the fathers of our country, both provincially and in Ottawa to find out why the U.S. has a rule to make it difficult for Canadians to entertain in their country.

Politicians don't understand

They answered me that this was the U.S. policy and they couldn't dictate policy to the U.S. I agreed with this, but I wrote them again and told them that there were a number of American entertainers coming into our country and infringing on the Canadian musician's employment rights. They scoffed at the very idea of music being called 'employment.' Yet Saskatchewan and Manitoba were thick with American entertainers coming in all the time, especially to Regina, Winnipeg, Kenosee Lake, Estevan Park Pavilion, Clear Lake, etc., These places employed mostly American bands all summer. The only answer I ever got from the government was that they'd look into it.

However, to this day – and that's 50-odd years ago – I don't see any results of them doing any questioning and the U.S. entertainers are still scrambling over our country. I suggested reciprocal programs, so that the U.S. entertainers could come here and we go there. This sparked replies like, "Who do you think you are? Those American bands are 'good." "Why shouldn't they come over here, we want American bands."

Are they kidding!

Canada had good bands, as good as anything that came in from the United States. In fact, most of the Canadian bands were more refined and still are. When I was first trying to get some government action – even interest – we had too many good orchestras in the Yorkton area alone to keep them all going full-time without having to compete with the influx of American bands taking our livelihood right out from under us, while none of us could go across to their country.

When I really pushed the issue, I've had some politicians tell me, "it's not important, John. If you guys can't make a living in music, then get a different job."

Sure, that's what most of those great top-notch entertainers of that day did and then our entertainment scene was completely dominated by Americans until there were almost no professional entertainers left.

I knew we had a tough battle on our hands, but being young, I was still willing to fight, but the problem was two-fold, there were the people in government to convince and there were the orchestras bickering among themselves, mostly over petty things that didn't matter anyhow. So what was more important . . . to make a buck and live or get involved in a never ending round of political debate?

When the Unemployment Insurance Commission began, we went on many occasions to government to discuss our problems, but were refused flatly. We insisted that we should be able to buy stamps and be entitled to the same benefits as anyone else. But their answer was that we only played (worked) 4 ½ hours daily. Travelling time could not be included, neither could the rehearsal hours, nor time spent booking and preparing. They said we were in a totally different category and were not eligible to pay for stamps or even collect insurance if the going got tough.

With the information (or should I say misinformation) that I acquired from trying to get on records and play across the line, human nature worked on me and every chance I got. In the course of conversation with people from various walks of life who questioned us on the subject of recording, we would deliberately try to work in our pet peeves, "We're Canadian, people think we're not good enough, can't get on records and can't play in the U.S."

However, I found out later that the average person doesn't really care unless something hurts them directly.

If government didn't understand our plight – how could the average citizen. The public just looked at "Canadian entertainers" as being jealous of the Americans and thought that if they supported us that we could eventually deprive them of the American entertainment they loved so much.

Many musicians approached me after I returned from Nashville to find out what it was like "out there," and I was point blank with most of them. I related to them just what I had observed. I brought out a few pointers I'd picked up and I also tried to point out to them that in many ways we Canadian musicians were superior to the Grand Ole Opry musicians. For example, our guitar players used closed rhythm chords, the American were still using open chords which we'd discarded. We modulated. We employed string, wind, brass, reed, percussion, etc., in our orchestras. We had definite patterns in our playing. Then on the other hand, the American musicians had better stage personalities, they wrote their own songs, put more enthusiasm into their work and were optimistic . . . no matter what.

The Canadian musicians would scoff, laugh and criticize each other while the American musicians would introduce, brag-up and bring on his co-musician with a big round of applause – even if he happened to think the fellow couldn't sing. From my experience, I found that we Canadian musicians, generally speaking, were – and still are – very petty minded and egotistical. Our attitude seems to be, because we can play a few tunes, get a few pats on the back for our work, that we are indispensable. Yet we desperately lack the intestinal fortitude to get out there in the front row from day to day, regardless of the drawbacks, public slander, or financial difficulties to perpetuate our talents.

We seemed to want to be second, not first. We always feel the other guy from the other country is better but when he does take the initiative, we're the first to criticize. Where did we inherit the idea we're second best? Why do our friends and neighbors across the line feel this way about us? Every time I hear someone say "You sound just like so and so" who perhaps started singing 10 years later than I did, my flesh crawls. I like to think I'm myself and I learned early in this business that originality is the most – if not the only - valuable thing an entertainer needs to be successful.

I tried to tell my fellow Canadians that we could play circles around those fellows from the U.S. The answer I got back from them was, "Ah, come on, it can't be." They made themselves believe that the Nashville musicians were automatically better, no matter what anyone said.

What can you do? You can't argue with people whose minds are closed.

I found this very frustrating. And I still do. But I don't know that it is ever going to change.

I still find it unfortunate that Canadians, to be successful, have to go to the U.S. to make it big.

I am more than 80 years-old now, and I won't be continuing this battle. But one day I am sure someone will maybe find a politician with a streak of patriotism and an understanding that entertainment is a business. In fact, it is big business.

13

BUYING A RADIO STATION

Managing the group got to be burdensome to say the least. One problem that I wish I could stop with the group was the drinking. It just didn't ease up. Many times it was heartbreaking to see such talented fellows making fools of themselves and me. At first I felt it was "our" band and not "my" band, so I let the boys do as they saw fit. But then I found people were saying "Smilin' Johnnie was drunk at such and such a place." It wasn't me at all, but one of the group. But mine was the name they remembered.

This is when I suggested they refrain from drinking before we got a bad reputation. I tried to be diplomatic about the whole situation. It would slow down for a while, but gradually they'd be back at it again.

It finally got to the point where I'd scold them and they'd be fine and leave the booze alone for about a week. Then just when I thought things were improving, they'd be back at it.

Under the resulting pressure I was driven to the point where, after several warnings, I just let the whole group go in late 1948 early 1949. All I had left was my morning show. This was a very bitter pill to swallow, but something had to be done and I fired them all as a last resort.

Buying a radio station

I kept singing on my Saturday morning show with the requests coming in as always. I shed the idea of any more groups. Although I was getting many requests to go on the road, I refused them all. The memory was too fresh in my mind of what a good solid group we could have had if I could have had the supernatural power to discipline them.

My nerves were getting a well-deserved rest. I paid more regular visits to my folks' business in Wroxton. I had more time to do what I wanted to do rather than work under pressure as I had been, just like a fox without the hounds chasing him. I paid visits to other businessmen around only to find that they were in the same kind of rat race I'd just got out of. Also I spent more time in the CJGX studio and for a while it was just like a vacation, except for the memories of all the good times we'd had on the road.

One day, Bill Liska called me over to his office and we sat there talking. He had more questions than usual and I felt a bit uneasy, so I asked him why all the questions. "Well." he said, "how would you like to be a partner in a radio station?" Being production manager at CJGX, Mr. Liska knew the business end of radio and Dave Glass the CJGX engineer was willing to look after the technical end of it. After much deliberation, they asked me in as a partner to look after selling and promotion and make the project complete.

Figures were brought out and they asked if I was able to put up my share of the money, and do my part to get it on the road. We needed something like $40,000 to start-up the station. We had about half of it ourselves and if we squeezed hard we would have had about 55 per cent controlling interest. For the rest of the money we would have to sell shares.

It had taken hours and hours for Bill Liska to prepare the commercial end of it to be presented to the BBG (Board of Broadcast Governors), the programming had to be just right.

Dave Glass spent hours figuring out the engineering end of the station. It was to be a one-unit, one-floor affair with a full plate glass front window where every announcer would be visible in action, especially from Studio A.

The automatic transmitter was to be the first of its kind. We would have had many more "firsts." I might also mention that about this time the wire and tape recorders were being introduced into the market and we were going to take advantage of these in a big way to modernize and improve the programming. I was to be in the sales field as well as supply a house band and look after live entertainment. All the details were settled, but the question was "Where?"

Smilin' Johnnie

Bill Liska was the key pillar in this idea, then Dave Glass and then myself. We naturally let Bill lead the way. He was the most knowledgeable. He suggested three possible places. First choice was Dauphin, second was Weyburn and third Melfort. Dauphin was possibly the most logical. Before going any further we tried to decide on the call letters for the radio station, but Bill had all this planned. He said, "CJBD" and went on to say, "J for John, B for Bill and D for Dave (or Dauphin)."

Since I had a new car, we would use it to drive to Dauphin and see the Board of Trade and various organizations and possible shareholders. This took many time-consuming trips because many questions had to be answered. Some of these answers had to come from the BBG in Ottawa, so we had to leave things in the hands of lawyers because we were still employed by CJGX and Dauphin was a pretty close neighbor. All our work had to be done on off-duty time.

While we were preparing to (hopefully) open a radio station in Dauphin, Ken Parton, the manager of CJGX started a strong program of transcribing live orchestras in the GX studios, making use of them on transcriptions and selling these to different sponsors for a fee. In return the station would book the bands on their own expense, pay their wages and keep the door receipts, absorbing the profit or loss. Mr. Parton had this deal going with the Cowboy Kings, sponsored by Massey Harris, and it came off to a good start. The transcriptions were in turn played on CJGX, and I understand that they were also sold to CFQC in Saskatoon, CKRM in Regina, CHAB in Moose Jaw and Brandon. This gave the Cowboy Kings a tremendous amount of publicity. Needless to say, my heart still had some spark left for music and after seeing what the Cowboy Kings had for music, and seeing what they were getting, I was left sort of down in the dumps.

I knew that our Prairie Pals could have had the same chance. Possibly even better, because we were a well-matched band. It was just that the bottle got in the way. Mind you, the same thing happened to the Cowboy Kings and many other groups and that's the sad part of it.

Sure enough, one day, Mr. Parton called me into his office and offered me what he said was a good deal with IHC sponsoring a group, but he said they didn't wish to conflict with the Cowboy Kings, so would I get up a modern band?

Really, I hadn't planned on starting up another band so soon and had never planned on starting up a modern band. Looking back on it, this was a mistake. However, I said I would let him know and went to see Bill Liska, and see what

Buying a radio station

he thought of the idea. Bill thought it might be okay, and might bring in a few dollars. Then in the fall we could just move to our station and I could drop this group, or pass it on to someone else, or if it paid that well I could always be a silent partner in the radio station venture and still play.

So, I went back to Mr. Parton and accepted his offer, and here I made another mistake. We did not sign a contract. Everything was verbal. Mr. Parton suggested that I get a new car, so I went and bought a 1949 seven-passenger limousine. Then I went out searching for musicians to form a modern band.

It didn't bother me that the deal I had with Mr. Parton was verbal. I was just happy to be part of the deal. I took the man at his word. My job was to pay all the wages and expenses and once a month present the bills to the radio station and be reimbursed.

We formed our band with Bill Devores on saxophone and clarinet, Mike Devores on accordion, Dennis Armstrong on piano and drums, Nick Woronuik on trumpet and fiddle and myself on bass and guitar. Though this group was very good, many people who were used to our previous band did not readily accept us and we had to start all over again building up new fans.

The station didn't know the first thing about booking, and on many occasions they would just send out 10 or 12 posters and a note saying Smilin' Johnnie is going to play for you. The hall would be booked for some other event and we would not be able to get in. In the meantime, these musicians of mine were supposed to be getting $75 per week.

That amounted to $300 per week for wages alone. The car, still on warranty (that was a laugh), was giving me trouble and the Chrysler people wouldn't do a thing about it. I didn't have the knowledge then, nor the experience, to know how to get after them. To top it all off, the weather was bad. It was one of those tough winters and the spring was wet and snowy. I recall on June 12 the E.J. Casey show tents in Gainsboro collapsed under about 10 inches of snow. This is what we were continually dealing with.

Several times I went to the station, but I could never see Mr. Parton, he was always away on business to either Winnipeg, Chicago or elsewhere. Paying wages and expenses without being reimbursed was making a big hole in my savings that were earmarked for our radio station project in Dauphin. However, I was sure Mr. Parton would come through with the reimbursement soon.

My musicians were getting uneasy and Bill Devores just took off one day, so

Smilin' Johnnie

I decided it was time to go to Yorkton and get Mr. Parton to pay me what the station owed me at least. I was getting fed-up. Just a few short months ago, I'd let a whole group go on account of their drinking problem, now I had fellows who didn't drink, but no crowds, poor bookings and no station interest, poor weather and disinterested musicians.

However, when I got to Yorkton, I was hardly half-way up the stairs in the Smith & McKay Building, when Mr. Liska noticed me and quickly whisked me into his office.

More trouble. The big boys from Chicago had some suspicions and they came in without notice and asked Mr. Parton for the key to his office. It seemed that the shareholders had a suspicion that Mr. Parton was using station facilities and bands for his own profit and I heard he was not just fired, but asked to leave immediately so they could check all the books. My heart sank, the few dollars I did have saved were gone with no hope of reimbursement. Mr. Liska had tried to get hold of me, but was unable. He was afraid that if the shareholders found out about our plans for the station in Dauphin he'd be fired also, and he had a family to look after and needed his job even though he wasn't well paid.

The same went for Dave Glass. They both asked me to keep the radio station deal in Dauphin hushed up - at least until the shareholders from CJGX were gone and all this trouble had blown over.

Through the course of our correspondence with the BBG they had sent a duplicate copy of information regarding the possible revenue of a small station.

One copy had gone to our lawyer and somehow one copy had got into the hands of Mr. Parton just before all this happened. Although I don't think Mr. Parton knew who got the ball rolling, he took this information to the businessmen in Dauphin, and by now they were quite interested in a radio station, so he started selling shares. The businessmen had all the plans for the studio and transmitter so it was just a matter of promoting the idea. Hearing this, Mr. Liska and Mr. Glass had no choice but keep on working at their jobs, disheartened that all their work had come to this. As for me, I tried to patch up the group I had and keep them on the road. But musicians kept dropping off one by one. One would quit, I'd hire someone then another would quit. The musicians just couldn't seem to get along with each other, or with me.

Some were only interested in money. Some were lazy. I just couldn't find the matched group that I'd had before, but we carried on.

14

4 1/2 DAYS WITH NOTHING TO EAT

My management problems at first probably arose from the fact that I was the youngest member of the group, 10 years younger than the musicians. I must admit it is much harder to maintain control over a group of men when you're younger than they are. However, at one time, we did come to a point where we had a full group but they couldn't get along among themselves.

With the shake-up at CJGX and the loss of my personal finances keeping a group going on the road was rough.

The group now consisted of Nick Woronuik on fiddle and trumpet, Ray Pasloske on drums, Ray McNeil on saxophone and clarinet and myself. We worked the prairies, but with all my problems, personal and otherwise, I decided to go out east. We played a number of radio stations on our way out, and many halls and theatres throughout Manitoba, Ontario and Quebec.

The roads were in very bad shape. We went through Winnipeg, Kenora, Fort William, Nipigon, Longlac, Hearst, Kapuskasing and right to Rouyn. Many places we drove over 100 miles where not a soul lived along the road. The police kept guard, you had to report to them before you left and again when you reached your destination. We found the east a little more entertainment-minded, and there was an acceptance of groups, especially in Quebec. We noticed a marked difference in Quebec, even though we couldn't speak French, we found jobs fairly easy to get. The people were more outgoing, they accepted Canadian entertainment with open arms.

Radio time was not hard to come by, even on short notice. Because of this, we spent the fall and most of the winter in Quebec, until lenten season, then - as in previous years - it seemed everything came to a sudden halt. We couldn't find anyone interested in booking us so we went back home to Saskatchewan.

When we got back to Saskatchewan, the two Ray's left to get other jobs, and Nick and I sat it out for a few weeks, then started re-organizing. Hiring musicians again, we added Garnet Clark on steel guitar, Victor Bjork on chromatic accordion and a little later, Wilf Wowchuk on bass fiddle. With this basic we started the '50's. Once in a while one would quit and another would come along, but this was the way it began.

Everyone hates the boss, whether it be the boss on the construction job, the boss in a printing press, the hockey coach, the office manager, or what have you, so it is in the music business. The musicians automatically assume that the boss is someone to resist. All he does is make rules and regulations, cheat them in their pay and make a pot full of money.

It's not really like that, but perception is reality and I fell into this boss category with my musicians and I hated it, because in our first group we'd all pulled together (at first). When I noticed the boys drinking, I thought, "Oh no, not again," but felt maybe I'd made a mistake with the first group by not drinking with them and not being "one of the boys." So I was determined to do it differently this time and lean towards them a little more. I thought perhaps in this way I'd have more of an idea what was going on in their minds and how they felt, so I gradually chipped in my share. The boys claimed that wine was a good stimulant and not as hard to control as whiskey. So I agreed and we started with a bottle of wine a day. The following week the boys said a bottle wasn't very much between five of us, so we bought two bottles. The next week it was three, the next week four, until finally our tolerance was built up to the point that even that wasn't much.

No one actually was drunk, we were just sort of stupefied. Within a short time the seven passenger limousine was pulling in front of a liquor store daily, (in different towns of course), and we began buying case lots. The way a person would open a bottle of pop, that's the way we drank wine.

A bottle each, driving along, eating garlic sausage and telling jokes. When the next engagement was 100 miles away we would drink two bottles each. A case of wine held only 12 bottles and soon we added a bottle of whiskey to sort of brace us up before we started playing.

4 1/2 days with nothing to eat

I don't need to say that this began to add up to an awful lot of money and with smaller crowds I had a hard time keeping up.

While in this condition, we played at Sheho. I'd had plenty to drink but after the dance some folks I knew asked me to come along with them and have a bite to eat and a few drinks. They had a large box of food and we were going to go out in the country, but they had a truck and there were four or five of us. There wasn't enough room for everybody in the cab, so I said I'd take my seven-passenger (it was still just like new).

We drove just a few miles out of town to a spot they knew and at about 3 a.m. we started into the lunch and drinks. The big box was full of goodies. Cheese, crackers, meat, pickles and a full gallon jug of home-made whiskey.

Well, we were pretty hungry, so we all tied into the food and drink using the seven passenger because there wasn't room for everyone in the truck.

I woke up approximately three or four hours later in the hotel at Sheho, in bed with all my clothes on. I was so thirsty. I just didn't remember coming into the hotel, so I quickly staggered downstairs to see where my car was parked. There it was, right dead centre in the middle of Highway 14, the main road through Sheho. I quickly hobbled over to the car, although I was nowhere near sober. I was shocked to see what was inside the car. It was full of cracker crumbs, odds and ends of meat, pickles and there in the back seat was the home-brew jug wide open with about a quarter of it left. The thing that really sobered me up was the cigarette butts all through the car and there were one or two cigarette burns through the fold down seats in the back of the limousine. Quickly I pulled the car in front of the hotel. Just in time too. In a few minutes the bus came in (the hotel was the bus stop) and it was followed by the RCMP.

After this incident I had to really fight myself. I was pretty disgusted with the mess things were in, but the first thing I had to do was curb my drinking. Then I could reprimand the group.

It was difficult. but I had no alternative. This boozing had to stop. Although it wasn't easy, there was no more booze. Oh, I drank after that, and still do, but not to the point where I've been drunk – and never on the job. It didn't stop the boys completely. They once again drank behind the scenes. But for a while the car had been a travelling bar.

Strange as it seems, with all the liquor we drank in the car, on the highway, we were never stopped by the police.

Smilin' Johnnie

We had been playing all fall with a five-piece band and were using two cars. The crowds were fairly good, but I had to spend a lot of money to pay previous bills. When December rolled around and things began to slacken off, we landed a job in the Saskatoon area. For three weeks or more, we not only didn't get the crowds, but the thermometer sunk to 30-below zero. I remember we came into Saskatoon a week before our Boxing Day dance at Marcelin.

We were all pretty near broke, but we checked into the Western Hotel (Wilf Wowchuk, Al Kinsman and myself). Garnet, who was a returned Air Force man, went to the Legion and they paid his way home to Cupar. Victor Bjork called some of his friends in Prince Albert and they came and got him. But the rest of us stayed in Saskatoon with no money to move anywhere.

In the severe cold, even the city was at a standstill. We ate at the fish and chip shop two or three times while we still had a little money. Their orders of fish and chips were only 35 to 50 cents and you got double your money's worth.

Eventually we ran out of even those few cents. We tried to pawn some instruments or microphones for even $10 or $15 until we started playing again. But we couldn't find anyone to help us. We even went to the City Police, to the Welfare, to the City Hall, but all we got was, "I'm sorry."

We had two cars and a full line of musical equipment, but we could not get five cents between us. Credit was not as easy to come by as it is today and debit cards were a quarter of a century from coming into being.

When the money ran out we spent four-and-a-half days in Saskatoon without a bite to eat, and I really do mean nothing to eat at all. We had access to water in the hotel. But who wants water when you're hungry?

Finally, on Christmas Eve, I found a man at the Esso service station, not too far from the Western Hotel, whom I finally convinced to buy the older car for $25. That's all he'd give me for a 1932 Oldsmobile in class "A" condition, albeit 20 years-old. But when you're hungry anything goes. Did that money ever look good!

We went to Prince Albert to pick up Victor and play Marcelin the next night, but not before I took Al and Wilf for a turkey supper. To our surprise, we had to leave more than half our meal. After not eating for four-and-a-half days, it was just too much for us.

The next morning in Prince Albert, I went to organize the boys only to find that Vic had organized three other musicians and was planning to take over the dance in Marcelin. When he saw us, he didn't know what to say. After some exchange of words, he did come with us to Marcelin, but with some of his friends.

That night we had over 400 people. The hall was full and by 11 p.m. Victor, our accordion player, and an important part of our group, was laid out in his friend's car . . . drunk!

Here we were, Al Kinsmen on fiddle (and he knew only a few tunes), Wilf Wowchuk on bass fiddle and me on guitar, with about 450 people in a festive mood, ready for action. Fortunately for us, the people enjoyed square dancing, so between square dances and a few songs, we managed to complete the night.

I mentioned before, that the government had a lot to do with suppression of the Canadian musicians, but the Canadian musicians didn't help their cause either.

These things happened in my group, but they were happening in every other group. The Cowboy Kings who had everything going for them, broke up at the height of their popularity and I haven't heard of any of them trying the music business again. These episodes soured some of the musicians to the point where they completely swore off music. Believe me, I often felt like it. The most frustrating thing was that it wasn't the poor musicians who drank, but the good ones. It was such a pity to see that talent go to waste. Perhaps they were drinking because they were frustrated with the state of the music business, and it was easier to drink and forget than to stay sober and fight. Perhaps.

Sometime during the '50's, I met Frank Callaghan, who worked for CFQC Radio (Saskatoon), and he was interested in our group. After some lengthy discussion I realized that CJGX was still a mighty good station to work with. In Saskatoon you had to be a member of the American Federation of Musicians in order to be on radio. You got paid union scale wages for your show, but somehow or other, in most cases, the stations always had a way to persuade the band to "expand" and buy commercial time on radio as well. So after all was said and done, you were still no further ahead, except for the publicity. That, of course, was at the price of the union scale fee you received.

This was too involved for me and it didn't make sense, so I refused Mr. Callaghan.

Not only was the deal confusing, you had to have steady musicians and they were nearly impossible to find. There was no guarantee from the union that

Smilin' Johnnie

anyone would stay the length of time you were contracted for, yet someone (namely the leader) had to guarantee a group and their work. I was concerned about this because in something like a year of operating a four or five-piece group, I would have musicians come and go. Musicians like Bill Devores, Mike Devores, Nick Woronuik, Denny Armstrong, Fernie Duplessis, Victor Budz, Jack Lensen, Everett Larson, Mike Derbowka, Bud Romanksi, Garnet Clark, Freddie Wowk, Victor Bjork, Al Kinsman, and that's just mentioning a few that I remember – the main ones.

Usually their reason for quitting would be one of these three: not enough money, woman troubles or the bottle. Sometimes it would be a combination of two of the three and in the worst cases some poor band member was having trouble with all three.

Smilin' Johnnie with his Edmonton-built Gaye guitar.

15

Giving up music - and life!

We had a few years of bad weather on the prairies during the fifties, and this wiped out many groups such as Glen Frain and his Buckaroos, Ernie Howard and his Farmer Fiddlers, Ken Peaker and his orchestra, Paul Perry and his orchestra, Smilin' Ernie Lindell (I knew he hadn't had the same teacher I had because he was American), Happy Russell (believe it or not, he was Smilin' Russell before he changed his name) Slim Wilson, Bill Smith and his JB Ranch Boys.

There are not many places on the earth that weather affects the entire economy like it does in Saskatchewan and across the prairies. Of course, the weather can hurt the farmer whether it is too hot, too cold, too dry or too wet. In fact, we demand almost the perfect weather to keep everyone happy. Even with all the technology and science and agriculture expertise available in the 21st century, Mother Nature can still rain on the harvest parade.

That rain in the '50s was unusual, for sure. Sometimes it didn't rain much, but it was never sunny enough for the soil or the roads to dry up. There wasn't anything we could do about it.

Farmers were struggling and the entire province was miserable. No one felt like doing anything. Neither did they have a lot of disposable cash to spend on entertainment.

Smilin' Johnnie

Smilin' Johnnie In happier times with his prized possession - the super 400 Gibson guitar

Giving up on music - and life!

The weather was extremely depressing. It seemed that the people were just too miserable and down to even think of entertainment. I was about the only professional dance band left.

The country roads in many areas were impassable, making it almost impossible for people to get around. Just a trip to town for the groceries was a major undertaking. Although crops were good, people couldn't get out in the field to get them off, so they rotted in the field. It was very frustrating for everyone.

In those early '50s, along with most of the road groups, I too, went flat broke. The finance company repossessed the car and all I had left was a Super 400 Gibson guitar which I'd bought new in Winnipeg for $1,150, a big Gibson amplifier which I still owed money on, a PA system, and a suitcase full of bills for car repairs, telephone, gas, printing, hall rent and many more bills to the tune of about $10,000. I brought all this, and Edith (Shorope), my second wife, back to Wroxton with me. Edith was from Saskatoon, and like my first wife, I had met Edith at one of my dances.

I do not have the capacity to tell you or to describe the feeling I encountered upon arriving in Wroxton.

My parents commiserated with me because the Depression Years and hard times were fresh in their minds. They helped me set up a store in town. The bill collectors were mad at me and used every trick in the book to try and get money out of me. They didn't believe I didn't have a cent.

Many of the musicians who had played for me called me a crook. What crime I'd been guilty of, I don't know, but I was (and still am), to many of them, a crook.

It got so bad and played on my mind to such a degree that I decided to commit suicide. I walked from Wroxton to Yorkton to see Dr. Michael Yoholnitsky to get sleeping pills for that purpose. He questioned why I wanted the pills so I told him. He reached across the desk and grabbed my collar and said "Johnnie, it's only money. Don't take your life over that."

Have you ever had the feeling that you were being continually kicked in the rear end, and yet when you tried to turn around you got kicked in the teeth?

My prized possession, the Super 400 Gibson, the envy of every musician around, I put under the bed, vowing never to touch it again. I had had my fill of music right up to my ears. I hated to do it, but I was giving up.

Smilin' Johnnie

Wroxton grain elevator can be seen on the horizon, and inset. Some of the houses in the village can be seen through the trees. Wroxton has been the home community for Smilin' Johnnie's family for over a century.

16

RUNNING A GROCERY AND A CAFE

I borrowed some money, and with the help of Mom and Dad I started a small grocery business and cafe in Wroxton. Many musicians kept dropping in every now and then, trying to coax me to play locally. My answer was always a very blunt 'no!' Red River Slim came in several times to borrow my guitar for prestige, but I didn't let him use it.

I said 'no' and refused to play so many times that when a musician would come into the store, I'd say 'no' before I said 'hello.' Store business was not all roses either, there was local competition and we were too close to Yorkton, Kamsack and Roblin to make a good margin of profit. Many of my friends and relatives took advantage of charge accounts, so on many occasions I had to pick up odd jobs loading and unloading freight, wood, cement, farm fertilizer or whatever, just to make ends meet.

One day, besides the usual round of bill collectors, my wife started harping at me. Then while I was in that frustrated frame of mind, John Mysko, who had a local group came to ask me to help him out. He was desperate for a guitar player.

I'd played for him before, and in my miserable state of mind, just anything to get me out of the store for a few hours, was welcome.

However, when I got on stage to play, what used to be as natural as breathing was difficult. I was truly out of practice. Such a beginner. Then a few weeks later, Alf Shingoose and Peter Khadiken came to coax me to play with them.

Smilin' Johnnie

I'd said 'no' on several occasions, but they kept coming back asking for advice, and finally I gave in and played with them - but only as a sideman. This I reasoned would give me a few odd dollars to put back into the grocery store cash register to cover up for the unpaid charge bills which were creeping up fast. Once you weaken and allow your customers to charge it just snowball's. It was much easier to play guitar than to load coal, wood or cement! But with the group, every little decision they had to make—they asked my opinion, and before I realized it, I was funneled into being the 'boss.'

Here I was, back where I'd started, being boss of a local group, playing within a 150-mile radius. We had Peter Khadiken on fiddle, Alf Shingoose on accordion, Nick Kozushka on bass fiddle, and myself. Martin Tkachuk from Scoby, Montana was visiting me, and brought his steel guitar and amplifier, so we got together with the band. Peter Khadiken was really interested in the steel, so the rest of us encouraged him to take up steel playing. I was impressed with the Fender equipment, so I wrote to the Fender Company in U.S. and got a small deluxe Fender amp—the first Fender amplifier in Canada.

The Fender Company was trying to get me to start a Fender franchise in Canada, but they didn't know Smilin' Johnnie was as poor as a church mouse with barely enough money to buy that one amplifier. It would have been a wonderful chance.

With the increase of playing jobs, charge bills increased, and so did the envy of many local people, who once again were saying that Smilin' Johnnie was making too much money! Here's an incident that will show you what I mean.

While in the store one day, a teacher from Brandon school came over to get our group for a dance. I requested that we get 70 per cent of the door receipts, but he said he felt that because Brandon school was the school I had attended, surely I could settle for 65 per cent?

Well, put in those terms, it was hard for me to refuse so I booked it. But when the dance was over they gave me 35 per cent and kept 65 per cent for the school. I tried to tell them that I'd been contracted for 65 per cent, but you couldn't reason with them. They said that was too much money for any person, or musician, let alone me. This treatment came from people I'd gone to school with most of my school days, and to say I was hurt just wouldn't be adequate.

One other time, Danny Romaniuk phoned me asking if I'd play guitar for him at Chuck's Dine and Dance in Yorkton on March 17. He offered me $25 as a

Running a grocery store - and a cafe

sideman. I accepted. A week or two before the 17th, Bill Cannon, who was in charge of the Wroxton Curling Rink, approached me to play at Wroxton on March 17th. After telling Mr. Cannon of the deal I had to play in Yorkton, he said they'd pay me the same amount and $10 each for the three other boys, plus $5 for expenses, if I would take it.

I was a little leery after the deal at the school, but since it was my home town, and I did have a business there, I phoned Danny and explained the situation, and agreed to play in Wroxton. The day of March 17th (Saturday) Mr. Cannon went to a bonspiel in Saltcoats and left two others in charge of the door at the dance. At midnight these two came and offered me $35. I told them I had been hired for $60. After a considerable amount of haggling, they gave me the $35 and no more.

During this period, many people came into the hall without paying admission because they were arguing with me instead of collecting the money. Both were inebriated anyway and in no condition to do anything. About this time, Mr. Cannon came back from the bonspiel, and when I told him what happened, he told me to quit the dance at 1 a.m. if they wanted to be cheap about it.

At one o'clock I announced the last dance. Then just like a herd of cattle, about half a dozen men (my friends?) stampeded onto the stage, grabbed hold of me, tore my shirt, and started cussing me, ready to knock me down. I tried to explain, but it's useless to try and explain to people in their inebriated condition, so I was forced to carry on. We played until 4:30 a.m. on Sunday. I paid the three musicians $10 each and $5 for their expenses, and I was left with nothing.

In my own home town that night, among what I thought were my friends, I was hurt and angry and figured I should have known better after the treatment I got at the school. In spite of this I still do business on a handshake.

Our grocery business started to deteriorate from the overload of charge bills. Local people would do their cash buying in the larger centres, and only stop in to show their face and buy a few odds and ends. Needless to say, I put up a good struggle before going broke again. I tried to play more dance dates. By this time Alf Shingoose and Peter Khadikin were gone, I used whomever was available.

Jack Lensen was back, the band he had been with had folded up and he wanted a job so I took him in, fed him, and we played whenever we could. For a brief period we had Albert Shorting, Vern Secondcost, and Corky Taylor. But these wouldn't stay long. They were after money, and money just wasn't there - at least not the amount of money they expected. For instance, Corky was only 17 and was still going to school and his father wouldn't let him play (during the summer holidays) unless we paid him $75 per week. Many a night we didn't get $75 total, let alone have enough to guarantee three or four fellows that much for a weekly wage, plus their expenses.

But the boss was always held responsible for the whole amount. I know that only too well. Some fellows that I wasn't able to pay at that time still wanted their money 10 years later.

SMILIN' JOHNNIE

and the

Prairie Pals

ARE AVAILABLE FOR 1957 - 58 BOOKINGS
"LET'S GO DANCING — WESTERN STYLE"

contact
SMILIN' JOHNNIE
Box 20
WROXTON, SASK.

OR PHONE — CALDER — 28r4

95

17

MUSICIANS 'THE WORST GOSSIPERS'

In the mid-fifties, we wound up closing the doors of the store, adding more bills to my collection, and heading west for British Columbia.

With me on that trip was Ricky Adams, George Gessey, and sometimes Jack Lensen. Jack would always join a new group, then when things went wrong, he would wind up back on my door step, asking if I'd take him back.

Sometimes I encouraged him to go, because I felt if he wanted to get into the big time. I didn't want him to miss a chance with some other group. He never did make it big, but he had a heart of gold and I always enjoyed taking him back – until the next time another opportunity came knocking.

We did some freelancing for a while. By this time, I had my wife and two small sons (age 4 and 5 years) on the road too.

Somehow or other, we decided after our B.C. tour that Swift Current might be a good city to make our base. I went to see the station manager of CKSW, Wilf Gilbey, who was very cooperative, but I didn't ask for anything more than air time, as I did not have anyone stable enough in our group that I thought would stick with me. However, we agreed on daily shows, and I moved my family into Swift Current in August. During this time, I had John Wingert on accordion, and George Gessey on lead guitar. Though we had free air time, people were just not moved with our music, and we barely made our house rent and groceries. We had little furniture and my sons Jerry and Bobby did not know the meaning of refrigerator until they were school age. The winter was a cold one, the bills were piling up on top of the old bills, on top of the old, old bills. Jobs were impossible to get, so by mid-February we moved to Regina by U-haul, with just enough money to put down on our house rent.

In Regina, we found many musicians who would play one-nighters, and entertainment was more in demand. There were more orchestras and more activity in Regina. There was Clem Gelowitz and the Happy Roamin' Rangers (top dance band then) and Ray Little's Radio Cowboy Show on CKCK radio and TV (which was just opening up). There were dozens of other part-time groups. I would book a place in the country, phone a couple of boys, offer them a flat rate, and hope that I had some money left for myself. During the rest of the week, I got myself a job selling Fuller Brush, door-to-door on a part-time basis. It was at this time in Regina that my oldest son, Jerry, started school.

We could not get on a radio station locally because most of them already had a group, and we had to wait in line until an opening occurred. I kept in contact with many musicians, orchestras, radio stations, and recording companies though, and we would have the odd radio show on CHAB, Moose Jaw. The pressure of rock music coming into this country caused an uncertainty in the country and western-type music that we played, so I decided it was time to switch from dances to shows.

Ray Little was doing shows, and doing very well, so I thought it would be worth a try. We began shows with Norm Mackey and Rusty Walker from Windsor, Quebec, myself, and Mike Rebalkin from Kamsack on fiddle; Peter Yatskowski (Noble) from Pine River on lead guitar started later on.

Though we all had some degree of knowledge of the business, money was what we needed to build momentum - and none of us had the money. So we just did the best we could.

Hal Lone Pine's group was working out of CHAB, Moose Jaw, and they started crumbling. Later on, Hal went back to the eastern U.S. Our group was pretty shaky and unstable. We were losing and adding musicians continually. The market just wasn't stable enough to supply a good steady income, and musicians came and went.

In Regina there were a lot of musicians, and their mingling would stir up a lot of conversation both good and bad. I've found that we musicians are the worst gossipers going! Everyone wants to make a buck and more bucks, so the information is passed around, each person is hoping to find a gimmick that will sell his band. It was in one of these discussions that I became

Musicians 'the worst gossipers'

convinced that I might be better off joining the Union (American Federation of Musicians) then I would have a list of all the union musicians, and when I needed someone, it would be a simple matter of dialing the phone.

Wages weren't a problem, since we were paying more than union-scale anyway.

It took only a minute to get my union-card and I picked up a job at the State Line Night Club in Williston, North Dakota for $150. I phoned four union musicians, and a few days later, after the advertising was done, we went to Williston to play the date. Mr. Christopherson, I believe, was the manager's name. He was a real nice fellow. Since I'd never played with these musicians before, I thought we'd better start a little earlier than usual and get a few things ironed out. Usually any musician worth his salt can adapt quickly and easily. When I had contacted each of these four fellows, they assured me that they were professionals, and professed to play anything, anytime, anywhere, etc. So we started.

To make a four-hour torture period short I can only say I've had better 'green horn' musicians play with me than these 'professionals.' It was unbelievable. I would say, "play *Five Foot Two,*" the accordion player would say, "Okay, I play it in key of C," the sax player played it only in E-flat, the piano player used only three chords for it when he should have used six, and while they were discussing what to do about it, the drummer would sit and bang on the drums.

It was obvious that these fellows were completely devoid of team spirit and just would not work as a group. They were just individuals putting in time to collect their pay.

There was no pattern to their work, no enthusiasm, no concern for the people listening, and no effort put forth. I was never, ever so embarrassed in my entire life. I could have gone to almost any little town in Saskatchewan, and picked up someone off the street who could have put these fellows to shame. I came back to Regina thoroughly disillusioned with the union, and determined to cancel my union card, as I had not yet been initiated.

Just at that time, it was our misfortune to lose our 11-month-old daughter, Marie. She died quite unexpectedly. Since I was absent from the music scene then for a few months, I cancelled the cheque I'd issued for union dues, and phoned the president of the local explaining my reason. To my surprise, my reason wasn't good enough. So I put it point blank — "I don't have to take garbage like that from men who think they're musicians just because they have a union-card." I went further and said that most union musicians (I still hate to glorify them by calling them musicians) work during the day and can only go playing on weekends and that's not any good to me, since I want musicians who will go anytime. I needed musicians, not labourers who work all day, then go out on evenings close by the city, and on weekends to pick up extra beer money. That's moonlighting as far as I'm concerned.

This was the extent of my dealings with the union. After that experience I'd had my fill of union 'musicians.' I'm not saying that all union musicians are like those I'd picked up, but I'm saying that the union should make restrictions and not accept that kind of musician.

Smilin' Johnnie, second from left, and his Prairie Pals, on a ferry in Vancouver, British Columbia.

Eleanor - and her dad - join Smilin' Johnnie Show

Eleanor in a borrowed hat and shirt poses for some promo pictures in Flin Flon, Manitoba.

18

ELEANOR – AND HER DAD – JOIN THE SMILIN' JOHNNIE SHOW

In Regina, I kept all my paper work, musical instruments, sheet music, etc., in the basement. One spring it was almost completely destroyed when the sewer backed up and flooded the basement. This was about the same time as my daughter died, so I stopped entertaining for several months.

It was difficult to get back to road work, but you have to carry on, you can't live in the past. I prodded myself back on the road, using whatever musicians I could round up.

One time, after having done a few bookings in the country, I couldn't get anyone from Regina to play for me, so I ventured out alone and started inquiring about a fiddle player. In a short while, I had George Dahl from Flin Flon, Manitoba. I asked Mr. Dahl if he knew of an accordion player. He said, "Yes, and I'll get you a bass fiddle player, too."

The accordion player was Mr. Dahl's daughter, Eleanor, who actually played more piano than accordion. And that was the start of a relationship that has continued for more than 45 years.

She didn't come on the road right away. But some months later, when musicians in Regina were getting progressively more expensive, I decided to write Eleanor and see if she was interested in trying music as a full-time job. Before very long, both Eleanor and her Dad joined me in Regina. We added Ron Rudoski

Eleanor - and her dad - join Smilin' Johnnie Show

George Dahl, second from left, with his band in the mid-50s.

on accordion, and with this group, we had to go back to dances. Dances did not improve because of the heavy influence of rock music, and the competition around us, it wasn't too long before Mr. Dahl went back to Flin Flon.

After all, he was in his late fifties, and it wasn't easy for him to keep up, although he often did surprise me. A short time later, Ron Rudoski also went home, and before long, Eleanor said she'd have to quit and get a job that paid something.

Eleanor, holding some paper flowers, with her Mom and Dad.

However, later in the winter, I needed a musician to fill in, and called Eleanor. This time, she said she wanted to come back and stay, regardless of how much money was made. After all the bad times I had with musicians over the years this came as a breath of fresh air. Someone who saw things with the same eyes. Jobs were scarce, and we were getting hungry again. When you and your family are hungry you get ideas pretty fast. So I came up with the idea of having amateur shows, something that helped us through rough times in the past.

For the rest of the winter we operated these amateur talent shows. We had no investment except phone calls, car and hand-made posters which were done by my wife and Eleanor. Eleanor also sold tickets at the door, and played intermittent music.

102

Smilin' Johnnie

Eleanor at her graduation from Hapnot Collegiate, in Flin Flon, in 1955, with her Mom Evelyn and Dad George.

I emceed the shows, and we paid the contestants a percentage of the door receipts, and still had a fair portion left for ourselves. And don't forget, the people had an enjoyable evening.

Our trips carried us farther and farther from Regina, and by April we had bookings as far as North Battleford and Meadow Lake. By this time, we again were playing dances after the amateur show, with Mike Rebalkin on fiddle and Bill Danielson on lead guitar. These fellows weren't at all consistent and came along only when they felt like it. Other times we'd pick up whomever we could. At this stage in my life in music, I'd learned to always keep my eyes open for opportunities, especially in new areas.

When we played an amateur show at Paradise Hill, Carl Hnatyshyn approached us to play for his rodeo in North Battleford, and an agreement was made. On the way back to Regina we stopped at the North Battleford radio station.

Being used to getting the cold shoulder from radio station managers, I was prepared for a negative answer, but I thought you never know until you ask. I went into CJNB, and it was there I met, manager Harry Dekker. After only a few minutes, we came to an agreement. The radio station was to provide us with a 25-minute daily program, plus all our posters, promotion and printing material, starting in the fall, and we'd supply the entertainment. I might also mention that Mr. Dekker was a swell fellow to deal with, an all-round great guy.

Eleanor - and her dad - join Smilin' Johnnie Show

That summer, we picked up a few Sports Days, and Stampedes, besides our regular amateur shows. Then in the fall, we moved into North Battleford. Here we started our radio shows and personal appearances in the area.

Once again I tried shows instead of dances. The group then consisted of Frankie and Louie Elek, Eleanor Dahl and myself. The boys only stayed a month or so, then they took off without giving any notice or reason. I was back to the old grind of looking for musicians. We remembered Jimmy Clayton from Red Cross, Saskatchewan, so we called him and he agreed to come. Then his dad got sick and he had to go back home. He'd only been with us a few months and we were sorry to see him go.

Eleanor toddling at two

Although we had a very good deal with the North Battleford radio station and were well treated there, the people in the city itself were absolutely frigid. We not only couldn't draw a crowd for a show there, but we also had a hard time making friends. A few businessmen were friendly as long as we were doing business there, but it was not a welcome feeling. The area surrounding North Battleford was not much better. We had only a handful of people who would turn out for our shows. Many a night we played to 12, 15, 18, or 20 people, and our admission was only $1 for adults and 50 cents for children - so you can see we weren't getting rich!

For a time, we were on CJNB radio, Monday through Saturday, and on CKSA-TV in Lloydminster every Monday (Lloydminster was only 88 miles away). We had the whole area saturated with radio and TV, but it was a red-letter day when we had 100 or 150 people for our show.

Eleanor loved music from an early age. Here she is four.

The $1 admission price was for a two-hour show and a two-hour dance!

19

GOING WHERE ENTERTAINERS HAD NOT GONE BEFORE

Looking to broaden our horizons we decided to try to get some dates in northern Canada, CJNB beamed into northern Saskatchewan. Letters were coming to us for requests from Buffalo Narrows, Beauval, Ile a la Crosse, and La Loche.

We thought we would like to go to play for these folks.

We soon found that entertainers did not travel into the Indian and Inuit communities that are so much a part of our country.

It was obvious that professionals did not travel into the north because there wasn't a dollar to be made and it would take them way out of their comfort zone.

But our idea was not to get rich quick, but to put on a show to please our audience and earn a living.

We put on the same show whether we have five people or 500 people. Most of the shows we later did in the Arctic and other far northern communities were the first time they had seen live entertainment.

You know most entertainers would not even look at making trips we made.

Sometimes when we started we hardly had enough money for gas to get to the airplane, let alone have money to charter a plane. We usually made a deal that we'd pay the charter on the way back and we never failed to do that.

I think the airline/outfitting companies who did business with us realized that we were not making any money at all, let alone making a killing. They deal with these First Nations people all the time and knew how much money they had to spend on entertainment. They also saw that because there were no other entertainers doing what we were doing and that gave them an appreciation for what we were doing - plus they knew we would have to use their planes every time we came back.

We made a lot of friends in the remote northern communities over the past 40 years. It has been one fabulous adventure after another and has given us not only a geography lesson about Canada, but a much better understanding about the people who have inhabited this vast country for the past 10,000 years.

It was the great people in these communities, who really appreciated our entertainment, who kept asking us for recordings. So once again we began writing recording companies. This time we got the addresses from the radio station, and knowing that there was no use in trying to get paid on a royalty basis we also asked the price for custom-pressing, in other words, paying for the whole thing ourselves.

Of all the letters we wrote, the most favourable reply was from Universal Record Company in Toronto. They said when we had a tape ready they would be interested either on a royalty basis or on a custom-pressing deal. We quickly started working on an LP before they changed their minds! We recorded it at CJNB with the engineer Bob Hildebrand.

Having scratched the surface of the prairie's vast north country from Buffalo Narrows to Churchill, we began getting correspondence from many places farther north where even radio stations couldn't be heard. These people wanted entertainment. The only obstacle was financing a trip of that nature. We weren't making any money in the North Battleford area, and were bound and determined that show business must pay off somewhere.

From all the letters we sent, and replies we got, we began to dream of a tour up the Alaska Highway to the Yukon, and thought if this trip paid off, we'd try the Mackenzie Delta. We were getting very encouraging letters from the Northwest Territories, but still it seemed like a dream to us. However, we didn't give up. We had entertainment and they were starved for entertainment - if only we could get together!

Just when plans were beginning to take shape, Eleanor began complaining about not feeling well. We suggested that she see a doctor, but she still insisted on working continuously. Then one evening at Alliance, Alberta, just before the show, she had to give up. She just couldn't go on. She was really sick with a pain in the stomach.

So we cancelled the show, and drove right back to North Battleford that night. Chuck, Luke and I helped Eleanor up the three flights of stairs to her apartment and then we went home.

The next day, we got a fellow to take Eleanor's place in the band, but before we left, the three of us went to see her. As we came in, she was lying in bed. We took one look at her frail body and darkish yellow complexion, and felt that the hours were but few before she would expire. Yet she assured us she was all right and didn't need a doctor.

It was hard for us to control our emotions. Even Luke and Chuck, who often disagreed with her, were concerned as we bid her good-bye until the next day. We managed not to show our fear in front of her. While Chuck and Luke prepared for the trip, I phoned Eleanor's landlady with definite instructions to get an ambulance and take her to the hospital, whether Eleanor wanted to go or not. I also phoned the doctor, and Eleanor's folks in Flin Flon and explained the situation to them. The next morning we found Eleanor in the hospital. She'd had a pelvic abscess and she'd had surgery. She didn't remember us being to the apartment to see her.

The doctor said that it would have been possibly three or four hours before she would have succumbed had he not operated. She weighed only 110 pounds from the hearty, healthy 175 she'd been before. The doctor also said it would be at least a year before she could go back to work on the road - if she would ever be able to play accordion a full night again.

Well, here I was, back hunting musicians again. I managed to get Jimmy to come back and help in a pinch, old-faithful Jack Lensen also filled in for a few weeks. Eleanor had gone into the hospital in July, and all summer we picked up musicians from everywhere, and of every description. Luke and Chuck never did get along too well. It was simply a conflict of personalities, so we lost Chuck.

Needless to say, with Eleanor in the hospital, our correspondence dropped. She was in the hospital three-and-a-half weeks, then was ordered by the doctor to go to Flin Flon with her folks for a complete rest. Eleanor assured me that as soon as she gained back some weight and felt up to it, she was coming back. She was determined not to quit.

Going where entertainers have not gone before

Smilin' Johnnie with his $250 1952 Buick Super on his way back from Red Lake

I was still using rented or borrowed cars, until one day while in The Pas, Manitoba, I picked up a really good 1952 Buick Super in mint condition for $250. I was well satisfied with it, even though now and then people would bug me about being years behind. This car was much better than many new ones and actually was the thing that helped put us back on our feet.

With Eleanor sick, our plans for recording were halted. However, we did make a trip up the Alaska Highway. I didn't use my car because I was afraid something might just go wrong. I rented a car and driver, but had nothing but trouble.

We were stranded half a dozen times, and ended up coming back to North Battleford by bus. On this trip, I not only played shows but I tried to make arrangements for our first trip to the Mackenzie Delta. We had numerous letters from northerners encouraging us greatly. The people in the far north had never seen a live stage show. A tour like this would mean real red letter days for the people at Inuvik, Aklavik, Tuktoyaktuk, Fort McPherson, and Arctic Red River. The more letters we received from the area, the better picture we had of what to expect.

All this time, our programs were still beaming over CJNB airwaves every day at 2:30 p.m. Sometimes we were actually there, but more often than not, the program was on tape. Sometimes we spent hours and hours taping one, two or three week's shows. It was a rough struggle for me, and perhaps it's only through Mr. Dekker's good nature that we stayed on the air. Although we never did elaborate on the number of musicians I would employ, I'm sure it must have irritated him to see us walk into the studio, new faces every second day or so! In the studio there was the odd disagreement, sometimes the boys amongst themselves, and sometimes with me. All in all, it wasn't for the benefit of my nervous system. Since Eleanor left for Flin Flon, I couldn't find anyone who would stay for any length of time and work for the benefit of the group. We had four musicians, but they were all going a different way.

20

TREATED LIKE ROYALTY IN INUVIK

I wrote several letters to Eleanor to see how she was doing, but she had drained herself so low that progress was very slow. She wanted to come back to work and was doing everything she could to speed-up her recovery. By the end of September she was feeling well enough to come home to North Battleford, and do a few letters, play a few tunes on piano for radio programs, and sing with the guitar for the show. I noticed a marked change during the month of October - the mail handling increased, it was more organized, and the boys behaved like gentlemen with a lady around!

We had the Mackenzie Delta trip all lined up for the early part of November, but I didn't think Eleanor should make the trip in her weak condition. I advertised in the newspaper for a guitar player, and found Guy Coderre from Dollard, Saskatchewan. He was anxious and seemed like a nice fellow, so I hired him. He came in by bus, and stayed the night with me. In the wee hours of the morning, he woke me up because he was in pain. That morning he was in the hospital with food poisoning from something he'd eaten at a downtown cafe. However, he wasn't held in hospital very long, just a day or two.

As I was making preparations for the northern tour, Eleanor insisted she would not be left behind. She said she'd been the one who wrote all the letters, and she'd been in on it from the beginning, and wasn't about to stay home when all the plans were finalized. I got her to check with the doctor, but when she went to his office he didn't recognize her - she'd improved so much since her release from the hospital. The doctor felt she was in good enough condition to make the trip north, so she did.

It was the end of October when we left for our first trip to the Mackenzie Delta. It was a beautiful Indian summer day - about 68F degrees above! Once again we were travelling in a rented car, a compact this time, but it was brand new. Since I'd been on the Alaska Highway only a short time before, I felt this was better than taking my own car. Believe me, it was crowded in that compact Ford. We had six adults - the driver, Eleanor, Luke, Guy, Mel Roy, who sold tickets, myself, plus all our instruments and equipment. We were to drive to Dawson City, and fly to Inuvik, Aklavik, Tuktoyaktuk, Fort McPherson, and back to Dawson City. We had - counting everybody's loose change - approximately $125 to $150 between us. I had $75 to last to Inuvik. We tried not to think about the money situation, or even what would happen if we got stranded. Incidentally, we did not have a credit card between us, either.

We were all in good spirits despite this situation. I guess we must have felt something like those who made the original Gold Rush treks up the Mackenzie. We were too curious to worry about minor details like money!

We had played the occasional Indian reserve and had been greeted with great enthusiasm by the people in the northern prairie provinces. They really appreciated someone taking the time and trouble to come and put on a show for them in whatever kind of hall they had.

Because we had to fly into some of these places and stay over a couple of days, we were dependent upon the local people for accommodations. They always gave us their best.

We arrived in Dawson City, on time, having had a good trip. But we were now down to $10 among all of us! We left our driver at the Bonanza Hotel in Dawson City, and went to the airport to see Connelly-Dawson Airways. At the airport we found that the Beaver aircraft we were supposed to have used was out of order, and they were flying us north via DC-3. Can you imagine the way I felt when I saw this DC-3 which was, as far as I knew, the aircraft I was chartering, and I had less than $10 in my pocket?

My only hope, was that I wasn't going to be responsible for the cost to fly this big bird to Inuvik. Connelly-Dawson assured me that the cost would be the same as quoted me for the Beaver charter because they had to make a side trip to Old Crow, Yukon with some mail.

We stopped at Old Crow. I kept this place in mind, thinking maybe someday we could come back and play there! None of us had done any amount of flying, so we really enjoyed the flight over the Ogilvie and Richardson Mountains of the Yukon and Northwest Territories. All this was a whole new experience for us and we even forgot the shortage of money in our pockets! I had left money at home to keep the family alive, and what little I'd taken for myself and the group dwindled pretty fast, even though we played some shows along the Alaska Highway on the way up.

When we arrived at Inuvik, we found it was a much newer place than we had pictured it. There were about 2,000 people, with another 1,000 in the outlying area. We'd left North Battleford in 68F degree-above weather, and in about a week's time we were in 35F degree-below weather. It was bitterly cold.

At the airport in Inuvik, we were met by Dave Jones from the Inuvik Lions Club, the most northerly Lions Club in Canada at the time and Tom Butters, who was the Area Administrator. It had been Mr. Butter's encouragement that had brought us this far north. He was interested in bringing 'outside' entertainment in for the people of the north. For us it was a great experience and great publicity as well.

The hospitality we received on this trip to Inuvik was like none we'd had anywhere before. Everyone met us with open arms. The people were really wonderful. We were taken to the hotel, a modern place with a café where the prices showed us we could not afford lunch, so we said we were not hungry, or our classic, 'we never eat before the show.'

From the hotel, the Lions took us to the Sir Alexander Mackenzie School auditorium. I could hardly believe my eyes. We were 1,500 miles north of Edmonton and here was a monstrous, ultra-modern school with an auditorium down the middle of it that could accommodate 1,000 people. Our prairie admission prices had been altered, and we had decided upon advice from Mr. Norberg, of Tuktoyaktuk, and Mr. Butters, at Inuvik, that $3 per adult and $1.50 for children would be a fair price. I might mention that this decision had been made by letter before we left home and we all thought $3 looked like a lot of money until we got to Inuvik. As a point of interest, at that time, eggs were $1.39 per dozen, oranges 49 cents each, a loaf of bakery bread was $1. All these prices were at least double what we were used to back in Saskatchewan.

The day following our arrival in Inuvik, we got a taste of what royalty goes through. The whole day was scheduled for us. We were escorted from our hotel in the morning and visited CHAK radio station and met Elijah Menerik the manager, a very fine Inuit gentleman who proved to be a very valuable friend through the years. From there we went to the hospital. All this was done in full stage costume.

We shook hands with the patients. Then we went through the hostels where the Indian and Inuit children used to stay during the school year. Remember, this was a time of the now much-maligned residential school. We were taken around the town until evening when we joined the youngsters at the Anglican Hostel for supper. All the children wanted to know who or what was Smilin' Johnnie!

One of the staffers originally from Pelly, Saskatchewan, had invited us to supper so that the youngsters could get a look at us. Those few hundred Aboriginal children tried very hard to look like they were concentrating on their supper, but their brown eyes hardly left us.

That evening was a most memorable one. The first time we'd ever entertained a predominantly Inuit crowd. The rumors we'd heard about the Inuits being very receptive were emphatically true. That night our share of the door receipts was $750 and the local people were concerned that we'd made enough so that we might like to return. Here were people who weren't envious of "all that money," but were concerned that we made out okay so we'd want to return! Our plane fare was paid that first night, and we were so very happy - not just for the money, but for the feeling it gave us to entertain these people who were so enthusiastic and appreciative. It brought tears to my eyes - after all the hardships and animosity I'd gotten used to - to see this auditorium filled to capacity with people whose appreciation, admiration, and downright love for us was so obvious.

It was an experience that left us with an undying love for these great people. It's impossible to describe the feeling we got from them. We struck a chord. They appreciated our coming to entertain them like no one I'd ever seen.

After that night, we were satisfied we could fly home again, we were so happy with our trip. But there was more to come. We still had three more settlements to play, Aklavik, Tuktoyaktuk and Fort McPherson. The next day, we flew to Aklavik in a Cessna, but we had to make two trips because the lack of space. Only the pilot, Eleanor and myself along with most of the instruments made it on the first flight. We landed in Aklavik, and it was there that I learned each northern settlement is unique. I was met by two young Inuits, and asked them to take me to the lady at the Community Club, whom I'd been corresponding with. When I got to her house, she didn't even say "hello."

Smilin' Johnnie

Then she said "What did you come for? There's no use to hold a show, there are no windows in the hall." She was very unfriendly. I was really shocked, and the young Inuits took us away. I asked them if the people wanted a show—and I got back a very emphatic "YES." So we went to see the school principal about using the school. But he wasn't too happy about the idea, and suggested asking Carl Gardlund, who operated a hotel, cafe, pool room, and picture show. If Mr. Gardlund wasn't in favour of renting us his show hall, we could, as a last resort, use the school.

Guy Coderre and Smilin' Johnnie with Carl Gardlund's wife in Aklavik in 1967.

In the meantime, Trevor Burroughs, the pilot, was getting impatient because he required at least two hours of daylight to make another trip to Inuvik and bring back the boys and the rest of the equipment. Remember, this was November, and total hours of daylight were no more than three or four. Here I was, frozen half to death walking around Aklavik looking for a place to hold our show that night. I met Carl Gardlund and he agreed to let us use his show hall. So the young fellows and I went back to the plane and unloaded the equipment so the pilot could go back for the rest.

Later, when talking with Mr. Gardlund, who had been in the north many years, and his family, I found out what people thought might have been the reason for the rudeness we ran into at the Community Club. Turns out there was a connection to the local agent for Pacific Western Airlines and we'd flown in with their opposition. Mr. Gardlund's little theatre seated approximately 135 people and the stage was the top of a pool table. The theatre doubled as a pool room during the day. The place was jammed. When we finished one show, the people would leave by the exit door, and come around and pay admission

Treated like royalty in Inuvik

for the next show! We held three shows and a dance that evening, and found the people of Aklavik just as receptive as those at Inuvik.

Many of them had put away their admission money the minute they'd seen our posters.

Aklavik was very rich in history. We had all heard the song *The Capture Of Albert Johnson*, but now we heard about it from Mr. Gardlund, who was a member of the group that brought him back to Aklavik after he was shot by the Royal Canadian Mounted Police after a five-week chase through blizzards and temperatures that dropped to 50-below zero. Johnson, nicknamed The Mad Trapper of Rat River remains a Canadian mystery. No one knew where he came from (his fingerprints didn't give any clues), no family member ever claimed the body, and during the man hunt the RCMP never heard him speak. He had more than $2,000 in cash and some placer gold in his possession when he was shot. It took nine bullets to fell him.

Mr. Gardlund showed us where the The Mad Trapper was buried beside a tree. He said he was so ornery even the tree died.

At Aklavik we found what we had been expecting in a northern settlement. Inuvik had been a shock to us because it was much like the southern towns, except for the prices.

Aklavik, however, had the dog teams. Everyone was in fur parkas that were locally made and beautifully embroidered and beaded with mukluks, in many cases, to match. This is what we'd been waiting to see. I'm not saying that we didn't like Inuvik, but I must point out that each settlement in the north is absolutely different and each brought its special memories. You cannot generalize and say this town or that settlement is typical of northern Canada, because there is no such town. But I must also stress that on this trip, Inuvik, Aklavik and Tuktoyaktuk became much more than "just another town" that we'd played.

After Aklavik, it was off to Tuktoyaktuk. Our contacts were Johnnie Norberg and Mrs. Helen Gruben of the Community Club, both Inuit. This was the only settlement (at that time) where the Inuit had made all the arrangements for our visit. These northerners sure knew how to make us feel welcome. Our accommodations were all ready, and the first words we heard when we got off the plane were, "Welcome to Tuk."

We were immediately taken over to Mrs. Gruben's house for coffee. Despite the bitter cold, there were people waiting for our plane, and they all rushed

114

Smilin' Johnnie

Smilin' Johnnie and Guy Coderre in the parkas they bought in Povungnituk, with Helen Gruben, her son and friends in Tuktoyaktuk.

down for the first glimpse of us. Once again we had a full evening—and all the people were concerned that we'd make enough money so we'd come back. The next day everyone was sitting around the Hudson's Bay Store. The manager said they were all wishing for bad weather so we would have to stay over another night. When the aircraft arrived to take us away—there was a collective "aaaahhhh" of sadness from the people who really did wish that plane could not have landed because of bad weather.

As we left each settlement in the north, there would be dozens of people standing in the freezing cold, waving good-bye until we were out of sight. This brought tears to our eyes. Every time we got ready to leave they would ask "When are you coming back?"

Needless to say, plans were already taking shape in my mind for a trip the next spring!

We had to miss Fort McPherson on this first trip, because of an unfortunate mishap in their settlement.

So after Tuktoyaktuk, we were winging our way to Dawson City, our faith in humanity renewed! These wonderful, enthusiastic, happy people made us feel that entertainment was a worthwhile venture after all. We had become the first touring Canadian country and western show group to entertain north of the Arctic Circle. And we did it at our own expense.

And this is as good a place as anywhere to tell you that our relationship with Mrs. Gruben is still going strong 40 years later. We last talked in the winter of 2005-06, spending an hour or so on the telephone.

Smilin' Johnnie and Guy Coderre in Fort Norman, NWT, with the driver of a Canadian-invented Nodwell vehicle especially designed for getting around in sand, muskeg and snow.

21

MAKING OUR FIRST RECORDING

After we got back to North Battleford safe and sound, we carried on our usual schedule, but it was awfully hard to get back to playing to half empty halls, after being used to packed houses in the Arctic.

We were already planning a return to the Arctic, but before we made the next trip we needed to make our first recording. After more than 15 years in the business and thinking that it might be a good idea to have a recording, the Inuits had made it very clear that they would like to buy some of our records. And we made a promise to them – and to ourselves - that next time we went back we would have some LPs with us.

We were playing our bookings on the prairies, but centering our attention on getting the LP recorded, because we intended to make another trip north as soon as we could.

Luke Jeddrey and Mel Roy quit that winter, leaving Guy, Eleanor and myself to carry on. We found it difficult at first, but Eleanor, who was recuperating 10 times faster than the doctors thought she would, was soon able to pick up the accordion. Once we got used to it, we were a solid trio. I thought our new group pulled together just as the original Prairie Pals had and I hoped that Eleanor and Guy would stay for a few years.

Once again there was a team spirit and a feeling of one for all and all for one. No one was looking for personal glory - we were all just striving to make our show a success.

Making our first recording

Our tape recording for the first long playing record (*Treasured Country Favourites*) was made right where we did our live radio broadcasts, at the CJNB studio in North Battleford with Bob Hildebrand doing the technical arranging. Bob was an announcer at CJNB, a real good friend and a terrific man for the job of recording. We considered ourselves fortunate to have him. Our record cover was designed by Glen McDougal of Fury Electric Instruments in Saskatoon. We had heard of Glen's work through his sister-in-law, Mrs. Jean Rolles at Snow Lake, who was Eleanor's cousin. She had shown us pictures of some of his guitars, and Guy was really impressed with them. Since Glen's wife and Eleanor were also cousins, we soon got to meet him, and spent hours talking shop and music with him. Glen was building the highest quality electric guitars we'd ever seen, but was suffering from the same lack of support that we were. Oh sure, many of the local rock groups were interested and bought Fury equipment. But the general public didn't even realize that a local Saskatchewan 'boy' was building guitars that were not only comparable to, but superior to the United States best guitar makers Fender and Gibson, both well known throughout the world.

Not only did Glen build quality guitars but he is an extremely talented artist and the only person I felt I wanted to design my record cover.

Glen took up guitar manufacturing full-time, but like ourselves, suffered a great deal financially because of lack of support. It was great to meet and talk to him. We bought as much of our equipment from him as we could because of the high quality of his work. But it was so disheartening to see such an enthusiastic and talented young man get such a raw deal from the Canadian public. It's just another example of Canadian attitude towards their fellow-man. It's really unfortunate that we are not completely sold on believing that Canadians are among the best in the world in many areas. Just look at our own music field. So many stars, but all have to make it on the coattails of the Americans, rather than their own merit.

When we had the covers, the pictures, the write-ups (for backliner) and the tapes made, we sent all this to Universal Record Company and waited. And waited. And waited. Finally, we got impatient and wrote to see what had happened. To our dismay, we found that the company had gone bankrupt, and our material was, who knows where? It took weeks, months, letters, phone calls, telegrams to various people to try and find out where our items were. After much diligent searching, we found all our material—the pictures and jacket front and back were at Modern Album, in Toronto, where they print album covers. But our tapes and masters were in Massachusetts. These were

Smilin' Johnnie

later transferred to RCA in Canada. We decided to get all the items together, pay for the pressing, and do our own selling. By now, many people in the North Battleford area were requesting records. We finally had to make a trip to Toronto to get it all settled, and before very much time passed, we had our first shipment of *Treasured Country Favourites* LPs.

Smilin' Johnnie playing an event for CJNB near North Battleford with Guy Coderre and Eleanor.

22

Airplane 'Lost' on Way to Old Crow

A s I mentioned, we wanted to return to the Mackenzie Delta in the spring. This time we planned to include, Old Crow, Yukon and Arctic Red River, NWT, as well as Inuvik, Tuktoyaktuk, Aklavik and Fort McPherson. On our way home, we had a booking for the Strawberry Festival at Haines, Alaska, July 3rd, 4th and 5th.

We had heard that there was a government grant available for entertainers travelling to northern Canada to entertain, so we applied for it to enable us to take in some of the smaller settlements. However, we were refused financial assistance.

June 1964, we were ready for another two-week trip to the Mackenzie Delta. We again chartered a Beaver aircraft from Connelly-Dawson Airways at Dawson City, and our trip was supposed to start June 24th at Old Crow. From there we planned to go to Tuktoyaktuk June 25th and 26th; Inuvik June 27th; Aklavik June 28th and 29th; Fort McPherson June 30th and July 1st; and Arctic Red River in the afternoon of June 30th. However, we arrived in Dawson City and found the pilot was sick and ordered not to fly. The next two days it rained, then in the evening of June 26th Connelly-Dawson got one of their pilots from the Delta to come down and take us back on June 27th. We left Dawson City early June 27th, thinking we would play Old Crow in the afternoon and Inuvik in the evening. As we proceeded towards the Ogilvie Mountains, I heard our pilot Blaine Wells, a young lad of 19, say something about "icing" and that he would have to fly at low altitude and change directions a bit. Blaine was used to flying in the Delta, but he hadn't done much work out of Dawson City, so was unfamiliar with the area.

We flew and flew with nothing under us but mountains. At one point the pilot, in trying to make use of every drop of gas, 'blew' one gas tank, running it totally dry. The motor quit. He switched to the other tank, but it took him what seemed like an hour to start the motor again! I looked at Guy, who was sitting up front with the pilot and his face was as white as a sheet. There seemed to be no end to the mountains, and no large bodies of water to land on. Even the other tank was getting low on gas. I asked the pilot where we were, but he didn't answer. I asked him again, thinking perhaps he hadn't heard me, and the answer I got was "If I knew, I'd tell you."

We were lost, running low on gas, in a float plane with no water in sight, and no radio communication. The feeling of "this is it" is impossible to describe. Then all of a sudden, in the distance, we could see a river and what looked like a small settlement. We thought it was Old Crow, that all this time our imagination had been running away with us. However, as we got closer, we noticed an American flag. That was strange. On landing we found that we were at the northernmost town accessible by road in North America - Circle, Alaska.

What a relief to put our feet on the ground.

The pilot had turned a bit too far when avoiding the icing conditions and instead of heading north, we'd gone west into Alaska. As soon as we refueled, we headed straight for Old Crow. We were way behind time, but there was no alternative now. People at Old Crow had been quite concerned about us, and we got the usual enthusiastic northern welcome with many willing hands to carry our two dozen bags of instruments and costumes to the hall. People who had been waiting for us in their homes began to make their way to the hall, and as Eleanor sold tickets at the door, Guy and I set up the equipment, so we could get the show started. Directly after the show we had to get everything packed up again and hauled back to the plane so that we could get to Inuvik before it got too late for the show.

I would like to mention here, that the people in many of the northern settlements are willing to lend a helping hand, so there was no problem getting help. The people of Old Crow wanted us to stay longer, but they also understood that other people in other places were waiting for us to come there, so they reluctantly watched us leave. We've made trips back to Old Crow and always have been

Airplane 'lost' on way to Old Crow

impressed by these friendly people miles from the nearest settlement.

We landed at Inuvik about 8 p.m., just as the show should have been starting. By the time we got the equipment loaded on the truck and down to the school auditorium, this being Saturday night, everybody had gone elsewhere. After all, Inuvik had a theatre, a hotel, and two or three halls, so people didn't have to wait for our show. We had a very small turn-out that evening. We were sorry, but there was nothing we could have done to change the situation.

Because Fort McPherson was planning a Sports Day, they asked us to change their date. We went right there after Inuvik.

McPherson was different from the other communities. There were no Inuit, but Indian people were very friendly and appreciative .

Throughout this north country, I was very impressed with their school facilities. These beautiful schools looked sort of fancy in comparison to Brandon school where I'd spent my school years.

From Fort McPherson, we went to play an afternoon show at Arctic Red River. The principal, Peter Torbiak, gave us permission to use the school, but said he didn't think we'd have a large crowd because all the people had gone to Fort McPherson for the Sports Day. We played our show to 19 people, mostly children and old folks. To my surprise, I learned that Joe Roenspiece, an RCMP officer who used to come to our dances in St. Gregor, Saskatchewan, was stationed here.

Due to bad weather, and the pilot's illness, we'd had to shuffle our dates, but this is a common occurrence in the north, and people think nothing of it. Radio station CHAK at Inuvik broadcast all the changes. We had planned two dates in each settlement, but had to cut down to one, so we could get to Haines in time. The weather held and we made it to Aklavik and Tuktoyaktuk for one night each. This wasn't nearly enough for them, but they understood. The sun didn't really go down, so I'm wrong in saying that we played 'nights,' because really at that time of year, there aren't any nights in the Arctic. The Midnight Sun is something you don't soon forget. It is absolutely spectacular!

23

WHEN YOU'VE GOTTA GO - BUT CAN'T!

We had agreed to give Inuvik another date, so they booked the auditorium there for a show on July 1st and a dance following at Peffer's Hall. Since Inuvik was the largest settlement, we had to bank on it for payment of the aircraft charter. After all, Old Crow's population was 350; Aklavik's 850; Tuktoyaktuk's 500; Fort McPherson's 800; and Arctic Red River was very small. But Inuvik had 2,500 people, so it was essential to help pay the aircraft to other places.

However, we found on our arrival at Inuvik, that the people in charge of arrangements had advertised our show at the auditorium at $3 for adults and $1.50 for children, and the four-hour dance at Peffer's Hall for $1 admission. The result was 75 people at the huge school auditorium, and the rest were waiting to pay a lower admission for the dance across town.

I was still willing to hold up my part of the bargain, so I phoned to see about the dance, but they informed me that their terms were 50 per cent of the door receipts for the use of the hall. That capped it. After a lengthy discussion, I told them, I could have played anywhere in Saskatchewan for $175 to $200. Their hall could only hold 200 people at $1 each which would give our group $100 for all our expenses. I tried to reason with them, but to no avail. I was losing money, and I was also pretty disgusted. We didn't do the show.

The pilot, Blaine Wells and Trevor Burroughs were waiting with our equipment on their truck, for us to decide where we were going, so I went out and said,

When you gotta go - but can't

"Do you mind terribly flying us back to Dawson City tonight." They were both a little surprised, but we were chartering, so they didn't argue the point. They took the equipment down to the float plane base.

Once at the base, Trevor said they had a passenger who wanted to go to Dawson, and it would mean $65 or so off our charter if we didn't mind taking him along. I was in no position to refuse a saving of $65 now, so I said it would be okay.

While waiting for the aircraft to be loaded, Trevor asked us if we'd like beer. I was so disgusted with the set-up at Inuvik and the night's engagement, I thought a beer might just hit the spot, so we each had a couple. Now, a Beaver aircraft has just barely enough room for us and our equipment, but since the passenger was paying full fare, I thought he should have the seat up front.

Guy lay down along the side door on top of the equipment, while Eleanor and I squeezed in and drooped over the speaker boxes. We couldn't sit upright, but we were in.

At about 1 a.m. we flew out of Inuvik, so disgusted with it that we didn't care if we ever came back – we'd be in Dawson City by early morning. After about two hours of flying time, I felt I had to relieve myself. Two beers took their toll. But where to go? We had possibly another two hours flying time. A few minutes later Eleanor said she also had to go. I said, "Hang on until we get to Dawson City." What else could I say? Once again we had to fly at low altitude through the mountains and the scenery was just beautiful. However, we were in too much pain to enjoy it fully. In the meantime, the beer was demanding an out! It was getting to the point where it was painful, and unbearable. I could see the pain in Eleanor's face as well.

Finally I said, "I don't know about you, but I'm going to relieve myself in my pants rather than suffer, and you might as well too." Imagine my surprise when I found that, due to the cramped conditions, I couldn't even accomplish this. We were sitting in such a hunched over position that our water was cut off! We couldn't straighten up because the roof of the aircraft was solid against our backs.

The pain got worse and harder to bear, until it was continuous. As the Beaver landed on the Yukon River at Dawson, you could see two people dash out of the plane, through the water, and head for the hotel, about a block away. When we got there, you guessed it, someone was taking their morning shower, and we still had to wait (modern conveniences)! But we managed to survive.

Smilin' Johnnie

We learned one very valuable lesson the hard way - never, ever, have a beer or soft drink before boarding a small bush plane for a long flight!

This trip to the Arctic was financially a loss to us. The people were very pleased to see us once again, and were very nice to us, the only sore spot being Inuvik.

In some settlements we did not deal with the Indian or Inuit people, Tuktoyaktuk and Fort McPherson were the exceptions.

After the problems we had at Inuvik, and the painful plane ride to Dawson City, we were pretty happy to get back to our car and leave for Haines Strawberry Festival. We also had inquiries from Fairbanks for their Fair, but we weren't a union group, and they weren't aware of the legalities involved in bringing in a non-union group, so we missed out on that job.

However, the Strawberry Festival people at Haines had a customs man on their executive, so they knew how to cut through the red tape and approved bringing us in without difficulty. If there's one thing that stands out in my memory of the Strawberry Festival it was all the go, go, go. It seemed these people never slept. A naval destroyer came in (we were pretty thrilled to get a glimpse of one - the first we'd ever seen) with 1,000 sailors abroad and the bars were open from 8 a.m. until 5 a.m., there was entertainment all around us. For awhile I wondered why they needed us. However, Mrs. Fox said they needed a family show, and this was why they hired us! One morning in Haines, I was awakened by my old friend Danny Romaniuk from Yorkton. I hadn't seen him for a number of years, so we talked shop and played a bit. Danny had been playing a bar in Whitehorse, Yukon when he'd seen a poster for the Strawberry Festival, and noticed that we were entertaining there so he hopped on the bus and came over.

24

TOO MANY PEOPLE FOR ONE PHOTO

From Haines we drove right back to Saskatchewan. We were using Guy's 1950 Chevrolet coupe since I'd taken the engine out of my car, and although it was a bit crowded, we didn't have any car trouble. The only trouble we had was with the people. They all looked at the car and chuckled—thinking what a poor outfit we were since we couldn't afford a newer car. I'll never understand why it is that a bank manager, a postman, a radio announcer, in fact anyone, can drive an old car – except a musician. The minute I'm driving an old car people think business must be bad.

We often took along a sandwich, or bread and fillings for sandwiches, but we had to make sure nobody saw us, because they would say we couldn't afford to eat better. Yet most workers carry lunch kits without fear of ridicule.

However, the truth was, we couldn't afford a new car, so we just had to grin and bear it. I often thought if I could get one of those old cars in mint condition, it would last much longer than the new ones. And I still buy old cars today.

Since our welcome had been so extensive in the Arctic, we began looking north in other areas of Canada, and the Hudson Bay and James Bay area began to bring some very favourable replies.

Towards the middle of August 1964, we decided to try the same thing in that area as we had in the Arctic. We would charter an aircraft and go to places like Rupert's House and Fort George in Quebec and Fort Albany and Attawapiskat in Ontario.

Smilin' Johnnie

But before we got that far, we had booked a fair at Emo, Ontario. They had contracted us for 50 per cent of the gate receipts because they were afraid to take us for the $375 wage we'd stated. When we pulled into Emo, you could almost read their faces. What kind of an outfit is this with a 1950 Chevy! However, we didn't pay any attention, and that night response to our show was terrific. We had asked $375 for two nights, and at 50 per cent we ended up with $455 for two nights. The people were a bit annoyed, but a deal is a deal, and we did our part.

The first stop on the James Bay tour was the air base at Moosonee, Ontario. We took the Polar Bear Express train from Cochrane, then we went on to Rupert's House and Fort George by air. It was a great experience. Once again, the Indian people greeted us with open arms.

At Rupert's House (now Waskaganish) there were so many people on the float plane dock that the dock sank.

At Fort George (now Chisasibi), we didn't have a wide-angle lens so Eleanor had to take two snap shots from the plane to get everyone in the picture. These people appreciated our visit as much as the folks in the western Arctic.

From the east coast of James Bay, we went back to Moosonee, then up to Fort Albany and Attawapiskat. Here again we found a friendly welcome among both the Indians and the white people. The entire trip to the James Bay area was drawn out on a map for us by Mike Pasko, the Hudson's Bay store manager at Fort Albany, and it was mostly his encouragement that brought us to the area. He was an enthusiastic country and western music fan, and I count him among my friends. We also met the staff at the Roman Catholic Mission at Albany, and they were really wonderful to us.

The Sisters made us a lovely lunch, and the Brothers helped us with our equipment. At Attawapiskat we were met by Father Daneau who gave us accommodations, had the show hall available for us to use, and just made sure that everything went smoothly for us while we were there.

I can't praise these northern friends of ours enough. It was through their efforts that our trips were successful, and we appreciated their help very much. It was doubly appreciated because we weren't used to people going out of their way like that to accommodate us. Needless to say, without the co-operation and help of these local people, we would never have been able to make any trips to northern Canada.

I might mention that this trip to the James Bay and Hudson Bay area was

Too many people for one photo

two years in the planning. First we wrote to clergy, postmasters, Hudson's Bay managers, etc., asking questions about population, halls available, accommodations and transportation. Then when we got answers, we'd try and plan our schedule.

In the Arctic we'd learned that it is best to make your deal with the aircraft people first, so we wrote Austin Airways at Moosonee regarding the cost of a charter. However, in talking with people in the north, we learned we might have been better off to take scheduled flights rather than charter. Even though we'd made a deal before coming to the James Bay area, we still had a bit of a dispute with Ray MacLean of Austin Airways that year. They'd sent a Husky aircraft charter to pick us up at Fort George when there had been a Canso going from Fort George to Moosonee the same day with plenty of room for us. However, after this disagreement, we became fast friends. We quickly learned about things like split-charters, and scheduled flights, and what airline company's could and could not do.

On the west coast of James Bay we saw tikanougans - cradles for babies carried on the backs of their mothers. They were made with a flat board carved ornamentally around the edges, then some sort of leather or canvas where the baby was placed inside, and wrapped up, and finally laced in. There was a sort of wire or curved metal at the top where they draped netting to keep the mosquitoes and sand flies off. Usually, there was also a shawl which was elaborately embroidered in rich colours. A young woman in a wheelchair at Attawapiskat had made us miniature tikanougans which we really treasured. We bought many pieces of handicraft from these wonderful northern people because they supported us to the max we thought we should return the favour.

One thing that struck us on these trips to northern Canada - both the James Bay area and the Arctic, as well as the far northern reaches of Manitoba and Saskatchewan - was the honesty of the people. They wouldn't touch anything that didn't belong to them. Many times our equipment stayed on the dock while we went to have coffee or lunch with friends, and the children didn't even touch it.

In fact, Eleanor left her purse with quite a large amount of cash in it, sitting on a chair in the Community Hall at Moose Factory while she was collecting admission at the door. When she left the door to change to go on stage to play the show she remembered the purse but she couldn't go to look for it until intermission. When she did go back into the audience an hour or so later the purse was on a chair right where she'd left it, on the only vacant chair in the

Smilin' Johnnie

hall. You would have thought someone would have at least moved it so they could sit down. But it wasn't theirs, so they didn't touch it.

I will never forget the northern hospitality, the open-arms welcome that I got from these people. Many of the older folk didn't speak English, but they came to the show anyway to listen to the music. If we played them a square dance, they were really in their glory!

I remember the first time we were in Fort George, we were asked to tape record a half-hour of continuous square dance music for the people. They had long-playing records, but there was always a break in the music and they wanted a half-hour of solid music because it took them that long to complete their square dance!

During 1963 and 1964, we had also flown to a few of the other northern settlements in trips of shorter duration—settlements that were not far removed from the prairies but had never seen a live show. We brought the first live show to places like; Buffalo Narrows, Beauval, Ile-a-la-Crosse, La Loche. Cumberland House, in Saskatchewan; Cross Lake, Wabowden, Mathison Island, Split Lake, Thicket Portage, Norway House in Manitoba and Central Patricia, Ontario, and a good many other outposts. Some of these places were accessible by a road (of sorts), others only by train, and still others only by plane or in the winter by snowmobile. We used every means of transportation invented by man to get to these places.

I doubt if we would have gone to all this trouble if it hadn't been for the wonderful welcome feeling we got in most of the northern settlements. Every place we went, the people would tell us of some other community in their area that would enjoy our show. Often we had never heard of these communities - places like Island Lake and Ste. Theresa Point in Manitoba, two places with more than 1,000 population!

One of the few boat trips we made was from Island Lake to Ste. Theresa Point, a distance of about nine miles.

Smilinè Johnnie

"TIPATCIMOWIN", Richelieu   December 1968, Vol. 6, No. 4.

Smilin' Johnnie on the cover of the Fort Albany Roman Catholic Mission newspaper in 1968.

25

'MOM IS GOING TO LEAVE YOU'

My first marriage lasted just a couple of years from 1948 to 1950. There were no children.

We used to get fan mail to the house and girls I didn't even know were writing. They would send cards and write "I love you, Johnnie." This used to bother my first wife, Sylvia.

I then married Edith in the early 50s. We lived in Wroxton and helped the folks with a café and a store. Jerry and Bob were both born while we were there. Then we moved to Swift Current for a time and then to Regina. Marie was born in Regina, but died suddenly.

From Regina we moved to North Battleford where Tammy and John were born and then on to Saskatoon because the oldest boys were in high school and I figured they may want to go to university.

When I came home one time my sons asked if they could stay with me. When I asked "Why?" one of my sons said "Mom is going to leave you." The two younger kids went with their mom and she denied the boys and I any contact with them.

Now my second marriage was about to end after almost 15 years. It was a sad time in my life. My wife was a good mom to my four kids and had put up with all my years away from home when I was on the road. I am not going

'Mom is going to leave you'

to say anything about her. When you live the life I live you really can't make judgments about a spouse who lets you live your life and takes on the full responsibility for bringing up the children.

Smilin' Johnnie and his second wife, Edith, at the funeral for their infant daughter, Marie. Johnnie's Mom and Dad are in the foreground.

When Smilin' Johnnie was at home he was Dad - not Smilin' Johnnie the entertainer. He didn't play the guitar or sing. On this occasion, for some promotion pictures, it was a rare treat for the children to see him in his stage clothes and with guitar in hand. Smilin' Johnnie's wife, Edith, sits with their boys, Bob and Jerry, while their youngsters, John Jr., and Tammy look on.

26

2,500 MILES TO FORD HEAD OFFICE
TO GET THEM TO HONOUR WARRANTY

We had a cancellation one night, so I came home early. I arrived at the house about 3 a.m. to find the lights on, which was rather unusual. My wife and two boys were down in the basement in about two feet of water - carrying books, correspondence, posters, etc., upstairs to dry out.

This was the second time we'd had a basement flood, and by this time, I'd lost nearly all my past paper work. What wasn't lost was badly water-marked. This was a real disappointment. We weren't living in a cheap shack, it was a three-bedroom home with a rental fee of about $130 per month, which was high at that time.

Everybody else on the street had blocked their sewer outlets, so the water had to go someplace. My wife called the city, but no one could - or would - help her.

When I purchased the '64 Squire, it was with a full warranty. The Ford dealer in North Battleford naturally wasn't too happy because I hadn't purchased the car from him, but I took it to him for warranty work anyway. After the second check-up, they still hadn't corrected the problem I had with the station wagon, so I wrote the Ford Company explaining that Victory Motors seemed to be giving me lousy service, just because I hadn't purchased the car from them.

The Ford Company's man came to North Battleford and they phoned me, but I couldn't seem to make them understand. They kept saying that I'd only had

133

2,500 miles to Ford head office

the car at their garage twice. However, there were three check-ups - after 1,000 miles, after 2,000 miles, and 3,000 miles, then my warranty was finished.

I was just trying to make sure the little problems were ironed-out before my warranty was finished. The garage people seemed to want me to feel silly about being concerned, so I decided to go right to the 'horses' head.' I booked two weeks in North Bay and southern Ontario area. After one appearance in that area, we drove right into Oakville, arriving at 4 a.m. or so. We flopped our heads over and went to sleep. About 8:30 a.m. I woke up, and without washing or combing my hair, I marched into the Ford head office. When the people asked if they could help me, I said, "You sure can, I've come 2,500 miles just to take a good look at the man that has the guts enough to say that the Ford Company has a 4,000 mile warranty."

Well there was a man there instantly. Before I knew it, he took my keys, and when he and another gentleman returned with the wagon, they had found even more things wrong with it than I had. They made arrangements for me to leave it at Dominion Motors in Winnipeg to be checked out and repaired under the warranty. Yes, the red carpet was waiting for me when we got to Winnipeg – but I had to drive more than 4,500 miles to get someone to listen.

It makes you wonder why people are so distrustful. Why does a person have to go to such extremes to get what he is supposed to get in the first place? I wasn't out to beat the Ford Company, all I wanted was what the warranty said, no more, and no less. Somehow, the garages always manage to make - or try to make - you feel that you're the guilty party. It wasn't really all that difficult for me to drive to Oakville, but what about the ordinary working man? He sure can't take his new car back to the factory and raise a stink. He has to put up with whatever service he gets. It's a shame, the Ford Motor Company (or any company that puts out a warranty) has the right attitude, but it's very difficult to find a dealer who will actually live up to the promises the company makes.

27

THE DAY OUR SHOW STARTED AT 7 A.M.

In May 1965 we flew to Uranium City for a show. Unfortunately, no-one had done any advertising so there was no show.

We were traveling in a small plane equipped with skis to land on the snow and ice that was still around in May in Northern Saskatchewan.

The next day we flew to Fond du Lac for an afternoon show and then went on to Stony Rapids in the evening. That landing at Fond du Lac was on an unbelievably small piece of ice. Bush pilots don't get the credit they deserve. They don't take chances, they are just so focused and committed to what they do. They know their airplane inside out and they understand the weather and the limitations.

It was after the evening show at Don Trallenberg's house that he told us "you missed the best place in the area – Black Lake." I should tell you that it was about 3 a.m. when Don, mentioned Black Lake.

You know when new places are mentioned an adventure is in the air, and we jump at the chance to experience something new.

One catch, said Don, the only place to do a show in Black Lake was at the school. Because the plane was coming back to pick us up at Stony Rapids we didn't have a lot of time.

The day our show started at 7 a.m.

Don said he would drive us to Black Lake at 6 a.m. – that's three hours from now – and we would have to play the show before school started at 9 a.m.

We loaded all our equipment into Don's 4-wheel drive vehicle and off we went. What a trip. It was just a winter road and the creeks were running. Before every crossing he had to get out of the vehicle to check to see that it was safe to cross the water.

We got to Black Lake and had to wake up the teacher. Then Don rang the emergency bell and got everyone else in the community out of bed. They all rushed to the school and everyone wanted to see the show.

No-one had any money. But that problem was overcome by Don, too. He went to the store manager, asked him to bring along his credit book, and then allowed everyone to charge their tickets to the store.

There were 100 in the audience at $2 a piece. It was a success. We were finished and out of the school by 9 a.m. so that classes could start.

It was a great adventure for us. We got back to Stony Rapids to catch our little plane and by noon we were back in Prince Albert.

This remains one of the highlights of our trips north. I don't know whether the folks in Stony Rapids remember it.

Later that year there was another opportunity for an unplanned show. We were on our way to Bella Coola in British Columbia, traveling over a very questionable mountain road, when we came across the Punzi Mountain Air Force base.

We stopped into the base and asked if we could entertain them on the way back from Bella Coola, such a lovely place with all the totem poles.

We played a show and a dance at Punzi Mountain and because of a beer strike everyone was drinking hard stuff. We always used to end our shows by playing *God Save The Queen*. Everyone stood to attention. One of the fellows had had a wee bit too much to drink and on the very last note of 'the Queen' he passed out and fell to the floor.

The following month we were in Wabowden, a place where we were always able to get a good attendance at our show.

Wabowden was midway on the railway line to Churchill. We travelled that line so many times we wished they had 'frequent flyer' points.

We got to know the conductors and the agents along the way and they also found a place for us to sleep in the caboose – a lot cozier and a lot more roomier than our usual bed when we travelled, the Mercury Marquis Colony Park – which we affectionately called the Marquis Motel. The railway conductor would tell us what time we had to get up and be out of the caboose, or we'd be rolling down the tracks on the back of a train.

On trips like this into the north we always got to know the other travelers. There's something about the north that makes total strangers talk to each other. You'd never think of talking to a stranger in a big airport like Toronto, but in the smaller railway communities and tiny airstrips of the north there is a feeling that you don't get in the bigger place. You are interested to know what draws them to the north, and everyone is interested to tell you and talk about their northern experiences.

But even close to home there are characters to be met and stories to be told. One of the regular spots we played was the Old Foxford Hall, nestled in the parkland between Nipawin and Prince Albert, a centre for the farmers from miles around, south of Wierdale.

In the early days – in fact, right up into the 1960s, there was no hydro in the hall. As crammed as we were in our station wagon we used to have to take along a generator when we played there. I don't know how we fitted it in, but we did.

Back in 1948 I played a dance in the hall with the Prairie Pals. We had more than 700 in there. It was a loud crowd, boosted by a busload of travelers who were stranded when their bus broke down close by.

Just to give you an idea of the revelry that night, local families the next day picked up beer bottles in the yard to fill a double-decker wagon box.

The roads in the area were not the best, even at the best of times. But our show always had to go on so we would get through no matter what. I remember on many occasions - because of all the shaking going on caused by pothole after pothole for miles - we had to make last-minute repairs to our instruments, as well as to the sound system, and the generator.

There was a different kind of problem with the roads in the Maritimes. We made bookings based on the roads being straight – as they were in the west – but many were narrow and winding. And occasionally to get from A to B a ferry ride was part of the trip. We often only had enough time to unpack before starting the show.

Roads in northern Canada were hard on the instruments, although winter roads

The day our show started at 7 a.m.

usually were a little less jolting.

One of the worst winter roads we ever traveled was from Fort Smith to Fort Chipeywan. Thank heavens we didn't use our vehicle. We were in George Mah's truck. George owned the theatre in Fort Chip.

We were seated four in the front of the truck. Eleanor held on to our dog Misty, but the ride was so rough that Misty held on to Eleanor – with her teeth and claws.

Eleanor and Smilin' Johnnie with the big, stand-up bass that was always fun to carry around in the station wagon.

28

Bush pilot flies us to 3 shows a day

The before-breakfast show at Black Lake is just one of many we performed that are totally unconventional in the entertainment business.

I remember one year in the mid-70s we were playing the Nishnawabe Aski Nation communities in Northwestern Ontario, north of Sioux Lookout.

We were booked to do three shows, but ended up doing 11 shows in seven days – and on a couple of days we did three shows . . . one in the morning, one in the afternoon and one in the evening.

All shows were in different communities and, all required a plane ride to get there. It was hectic alright, but it was enjoyable.

We chartered a bush pilot to take us to Big Trout Lake. We knew we had three shows booked, but when Johnnie went on the two-way radio to confirm them, other communities heard the radio discussions and wanted us to take our show to them as well. So there was no time for lots of promotion in these communities. We said we would go when they wanted us there – and that we did. In a day or so we were playing our show in small, remote communities, and to appreciative crowds. It was amazing how these communities jumped at the chance to have us entertain them. From Big Trout Lake we eventually played Muskrat Dam, Sachigo Lake, Bearskin Lake, Kingfisher Lake, Wunnemin Lake, Kasabonica, Weagamow Lake and Sandy Lake.

We'd get up, in the morning, fly to the first community, put on a show around

Bush pilot flies us to 3 shows a day

noon, then pack up and fly to the next settlement for a show late afternoon, then pack up and fly to another community for the evening.

We flew back to Big Trout Lake every night to overnight because they had given us a house to stay in.

There wasn't much time to eat during the day, so we would get back to the house and eat at night. Also, the day was so hectic, that there wasn't even time to count the money from each show. That was all done when we got home in the evening.

With all the shows done, on the flight back we were on the approach to the airport at Sioux Lookout when a private plane came awfully close to us. Our pilot said a few choice words and we heaved a sigh of relief.

We were glad to land and very happy to be in the station wagon again – heading this time for Saskatoon. It had been a hectic seven days. Entertainers don't live like this . . . except us. We felt very honoured to be able to play these small communities in this remote, but very beautiful area of Northern Ontario.

Little did we know that a month later we would be back in Northern Ontario, flying with an outfitter from Nakina, to other first nations settlements in Webequie, Lansdowne House and Fort Hope.

By now we had been able to reduce our accommodation budget because we had purchased a Boler trailer. This was our home on the road – at least when we could drive to our jobs.

We parked the Boler at the outfitter's office in Nakina while the plane was undergoing some mechanical work. Other planes were not available because they were helping to fight forest fires in the area.

We waited a couple of days for them to fix the Otter, but then as we were racing across the water there was one small problem . . . the pilot could not get it airborne.

Several attempts were made before we had some success. The pilot got it in the air just as I thought we were going to pile into the bush at the end of the lake.

As if this wasn't enough excitement for a lifetime, let alone a day, we ran into another problem – the plane would not gain altitude. We were flying just a few feet above the treetops.

We couldn't hear much of the conversation in the cockpit, but we did hear "I don't care what the boss does to me, I'm turning this thing around and taking it back before we crash."

Smilin' Johnnie

It was a quiet, white knuckle, and uneventful few minutes before we touched down on the lake. But we didn't mind. We were just glad to have landed safely.

We unloaded all our equipment and spent another night in the Boler while the Otter was back in the repair shop.

Next day we flew out without any problems. The pilots were telling us that the previous day's problems were probably something to do with the hot weather and the barometric pressure. Whatever it was, it sure scared us.

Then we went back home, moved from Saskatoon to the land near Wroxton – and our new life. That Boler was our home for a few weeks in the yard while we got the farmhouse fixed up.

The Boler became our all-weather home when we were travelling. With a little heater we carried it was warm and cozy even at 25-below zero.

Eleanor poses with a 'sold-out' show sign at Medicine Hat.

SMILIN' JOHNNIE AND HIS PRAIRIE PALS

The year 1967 is of double importance to Smilin' Johnnie and His Prairie Pals. Besides being Canada's Centennial year, it marks the 21st consecutive year that Smilin' Johnnie and His Prairie Pals have been entertaining their fellow Canadians.

Being a part of the entertainment touring business in Canada's great west and north has presented many problems that would appear unsurmountable to the average entertainer, but for the Smilin' Johnnie group, all the problems seemed to turn out to be great and wonderful experiences. They are probably the only group in Canada who have travelled to engagements by plane, dog team, bombadier and canoe, and by the same token have probably seen more of Canada than most groups. Their travels have brought them many hours of satisfaction, through meeting Canadians from all walks of life, new Canadian composers and entertainers as well as knowing that they have brought much happiness to Canadians who are in regions where travelling shows never appear.

Besides being the only Canadian who has been entertaining professionally in Western Canada for twenty once consecutive years, Smilin' Johnny & His Prairie Pals have several firsts to their credit including being the first group to bring live country entertainment north of the Arctic Circle and the first group to bring live entertainment to residents along the James Bay in Ontario and Quebec.

Wherever Smilin' Johnny & His Prairie Pals appear, it's a sellout. Newspaper, radio and television coverage is extensive. Their two hour show has drawn raves from residents from north of the Arctic Circle, the interior of Quebec and westward to the Queen Charlotte Islands.

Smilin' Johnnie, Eleanor Dahl and Guy Coderre, who make up the Smilin' Johnny Shows, have recently released their own Centennial Year project, in the form of an album titled "Smilin' Johnnie & His Prairie Pals Salute Canada's Northland" (CML 1065). Those interested in this album should direct their requests to:

Smilin' Johnnie Shows, 314 Vancouver Avenue South, Saskatoon, Saskatchewan

29

A POLITICIAN HELPS – FINALLY!

I went to Harry Dekker, who was still the manager of CJNB although the station had been bought by some new outfit, and asked him if he minded if we moved out of North Battleford and cancelled our program commitment.

I explained the various reasons—our usual program slot was sold to another group and we were on later, 3 p.m. to 3:30 p.m., plus the fact that we'd lost most of our advertising material in the basement flood, and we felt it best to move on. Incidentally, when the basement flooded, I mentioned that my wife had called the city and was met with the attitude which we'd grown used to in North Battleford, "That's too bad, (ho hum), you shouldn't keep valuable things in the basement." A complete lack of concern. We liked the area, beautiful river, rolling hills surrounding the city, but I couldn't say the same for the people.

Oh, we had a couple of friends, but we just couldn't make many friends or much money. Mr. Dekker agreed that there was a general lack of interest in the area, so we pulled out of North Battleford the first week in July of 1965.

Where does a person go, and why? Most people usually ask this question, and now I was asking myself – 'where should we go?' I'd been in Yorkton, Regina, Swift Current, and off and on in Moose Jaw.

How about Prince Albert? From our previous experience with Mr. Rawlinson when they'd purchased CJNB we had approached them about a TV spot in

A politician helps - finally!

conjunction with our radio show and his answer was "How long do you think you can stay in business, you've been around a long time already?" It was a flat refusal, so Prince Albert was out of the question.

I'd been all over Canada, our work was all over Canada, so we needed to be centrally located. I thought perhaps the Lakehead or Winnipeg, but I felt both centers were a little too big for me and my family to spend the rest of our lives. It was nice to shop in Winnipeg, but I didn't think living there would be right.

My wife and family suggested Saskatoon. My immediate thought was the memory of how hungry I'd been in Saskatoon and I thought it might possibly be another North Battleford, only bigger. But even Eleanor and Guy agreed that Saskatoon would be a fine place. I think deep down, we were all reluctant to leave Saskatchewan, we were all born and raised in the province and it was difficult to think of the Prairie Pals working out of the Lakehead!

Actually by this time, we seldom used the Prairie Pals name, and usually went as the Smilin' Johnnie Show. But it was difficult to think of tearing up the roots we'd put down in Saskatchewan. You might say our thinking was "Saskatchewan-oriented" if there is such a thing! So the move was made 100 miles, to Saskatoon, the city of bridges. It's a really lovely, clean city. I felt it would be a nice place to live for my family.

We did not, at first, get to know many people in Saskatoon because we just continued with our personal appearances. It was quite a relief after having done over 1,150 broadcasts on CJNB in the past few years, plus TV shows at Lloydminster, to have that extra time to use for promotion, booking and advertising. Three weeks after we moved to Saskatoon, on July 25th, while enroute to play a show around Raymore, Saskatchewan, on Highway 6, we were travelling along about 60 mph or so, when Eleanor said, "I smell something burning." Guy had the window open and he thought maybe it was the fresh tar along the road.

The smell continued for a few minutes, so I decided to stop and see what it was. I pulled over to the shoulder gradually, but by the time I came to a full stop, the whole front end of the car was in smoke. Eleanor hollered, "The instruments!" We still couldn't afford insurance policies so everything was not insured. I pressed the button for the electric rear window. Only seconds later the fire cut through the electrical system causing the horn to blow, radio to play, etc. We rushed to get our instruments out and in a short while, many people were gathered around with fire extinguishers, etc. The whole front-end burned though, and finally the people pushed the wagon off the road because it was beginning to burn the asphalt.

I phoned my landlord, Orest Missura in Saskatoon. He was about the only person I knew in the city. He drove out and picked us up and brought the equipment back to Saskatoon that night. The next morning Guy and I went to Saskatchewan Government Insurance office to put in a claim. I had a package policy, so we went in first thing Monday morning and explained what happened. The insurance man said, "Well, we'll try and have a man out there to get the car in a couple of weeks." Upon hearing this, I asked him if they could get us a car to use in the meantime, as the car is our livelihood.

I went further to say that we're not fussy what kind of vehicle, just so long as we can get to our engagements. His reply to this was something like, "Why didn't you burn the car up better?" He said it was impossible for them to supply a vehicle when there was no second party involved. I told him exactly what happened, but he still seemed to think we'd burned the car on purpose. At this point, I could see we weren't making any progress, so Guy and I left there and went to see a lawyer. After hearing our plight, he said he could write them a letter.

Here we were, walking around downtown about 10 a.m. wondering where to turn next when we came to the Social Welfare Office and at that moment, an idea came to me. I said, "Guy, let's go in here." We went downstairs and asked to see the manager, or boss, or whatever. He was very courteous and asked what our problem was and if he could help us. I sat down and related the story of how our car had burned up, and that we required a car to earn our living, but the insurance people think we burned the car on purpose. He said, "What's that got to do with welfare?" Then I went on to tell him what we do, and how we operate. I said, "Today is Monday, July 26th, I need a car to go to Edson, Alberta to play a rodeo on July 28th, 30th, and 31st. That money will be paying the rent for myself and my family, Miss Dahl, and Mr. Coderre, plus buying our groceries, paying lights, water and it will also finance our trip to Ontario, where we have a three-week tour. That three-week tour will keep us going until fall. It's a chain reaction thing, if we can't get a car to go to Edson, then we won't have enough for our rent, then neither will we have enough to get to our engagements in Ontario and we'll be destitute for the fall and winter, and will be forced to come down here for welfare to support eight of us."

Now the welfare man clearly understood my problem. He quickly phoned the Saskatchewan Government Insurance office man we'd just seen a little

A politician helps - finally!

earlier. I cannot relate the entire conversation, but I could plainly see that the welfare man was getting pretty mad, and as he hung up the receiver, he twiddled his pencil for a moment, then said, "Here, go and dial this number and ask for Sally Marchant, explain what you've just told me, She is our new MP (provincial legislature) and if she can't help you, come back and see me."

I thought, 'Oh boy, I know how much help I can usually expect from the government, exactly zero,' but I phoned Sally Marchant at a quarter to twelve. She listened intently as I once again told the whole story, explaining it in detail as I had to both the insurance people and the welfare people.

Sally said, "Call back in an hour." When I called back she apologized for the government insurance, and said to excuse her if she sounded a bit angry, but she waited through 32 rings on the phone before getting an answer at the Saskatchewan Insurance office.

She said, "You go there and see a certain man (I've forgotten his name) first thing on Tuesday morning and they'll have your car in by 5 p.m. today." She had also been in touch with Dominion Motors but she said the business end was up to me, if I wanted to trade. She asked that if I ran into any more complications to call her at the Parliament Buildings in Regina since she was headed there that afternoon.

I thanked her very much (she renewed my faith in getting action from the government people!). It was nice to have someone who believed us, and was willing to help.

Tuesday morning first thing, I was at Saskatchewan Government Insurance office. They had inspected the car and said everything was settled, "Go to Dominion Motors and pick up another wagon, same make and model." I had hoped to trade the '64 on a '66, but seeing as it burned and the 66's weren't in, I had to settle for a '65 exactly the same as the '64 with all the extras, but white with red leatherette interior. The deal I was forced to make with Dominion Motors at this time, wasn't exactly advantageous. It seems some people thrive on the misfortunes of others. It cost us $1,500 difference, but one must have a car, and financial losses have to be put aside in cases of emergency. Wednesday morning we were on the road again – finally, Alberta-bound to Edson.

30

POVUNGNITUK HONOURS US BY SINGING ABIDE WITH ME

I had discovered that if you get the right person in government you can get action. Why not try and get some action from Ottawa? The only reason for lack of action there was because we were the only ones pushing them for laws governing foreign entertainment coming into our country. I remembered the people up north, who were literally scared to open their mouths and speak their mind. Many of them hoped that we'd do this for them - but if we did - it would seem to be only one person's opinion, especially when I did all the letter writing and requesting. I felt sorry for the northerners, because even I had a hard time to decide who actually governs the Northwest Territories (at that time). I had written to many different people and they kept passing the buck. I finally wound up writing Ben Sivertz, the Territorial Administrator, but even then I didn't make any headway!

After leaving the prairies at the end of July we motored down to Ontario. In the past we'd found that in order to make these trips pay, it would be best to take a whole month for the James Bay area, and fly on scheduled aircraft instead of chartering. This year's schedule was arranged by Ray MacLean, base manager for Austin Airways. We wrote for our bookings, according to the Austin Airways schedule. All the places we'd written (places we'd been the previous year) were anxious to have us back, and we added some new ones - Povungnituk, Quebec, and Cape Dorset, on Baffin Island, NWT as well as Great Whale River, Quebec.

Povungnituk honours us by singing Abide With Me

Povungnituk was a conversation piece every time we talked shop.

Mr. MacLean insisted that we try to fly into POV (as the people in that area called it) and play our show. But I showed him the letters that I received from the RC priest there who painted a very bleak picture. Also, the letter from the Hudson's Bay store manager, wasn't very encouraging.

However, Ray insisted that we go. He was so sure that it would be successful that he said he would forgo the $350 air fare if we didn't do well. There was one hitch, we'd have to spend three days there to wait for the next flight out. But with Ray's assurance that we'd do well, I decided to take a chance on it.

We flew to POV by Canso, a large twin-engine aircraft that lands on its belly in the water. The Inuit came out in their boats, and we were taken to the dock. As we neared the dock we were greeted by about 200 ruddy, smiling, laughing, happy, chanting, Inuit people with open arms - wanting just to touch us to make sure we were really there.

It's a feeling that is hard to describe. They just seemed to absorb us and sort of melt us into their community as one of them in an instant. They made us feel at home. We were honoured and thrilled to be a part of these warm, happy, loving people. Our arrangements were made to play the show at the Anglican Hall, so I scrambled around the crowd looking for - and finally finding - Mr. and Mrs. Burroughs, the minister and his wife. They greeted us very kindly and took us to their house where we would stay while in the community. The Burroughs' had only been in POV a short time too, and were just learning the Inuit language.

We had many interesting conversations with them about the north and they were great folks. We got along famously - except when it came to our morning coffee. Being English, Mr. Burroughs preferred his morning tea, but he compromised by holding his nose while he brought us our coffee. He mentioned that it was fine to hold our show each night at 8 p.m., except Wednesday when they had a church service and would appreciate it if we started later. This was fine with us and I also mentioned that I had heard the Inuit people were poor, and we heard POV was famous for soapstone carvings, so we'd take carvings instead of cash if they were short.

The first night we grossed $345. The second night we did about the same. Knowing that the church service was scheduled the third night, we were in no rush to go to the hall and got into conversation about the north with Mrs. Burroughs. As I happened to glance out the window, I noticed this drove of people headed towards the hall which was only a few yards away from the church. I said to Eleanor, who was responsible for selling tickets, "You'd better hurry up and get over there to start selling tickets." So she did, but moments later she returned with the cash box empty and tears in her eyes saying she couldn't even get close to the door.

Well, we had about $700 taken in the previous nights, so I said, "Let's go on and give them a free show, it's certainly not going to hurt us to give them a couple of hours of entertainment. We played our show as always, giving our best to the folks, and after the show was over, a short, smiling Inuit lad came over to Eleanor with a shoe box. Eleanor thought perhaps he wanted to sell a carving, she opened the box and it was full of money. The young man couldn't speak English, so we quickly got Zebedee Nungak, who said he would interpret for us if we needed him. He was a real ambitious young fellow, and Zebedee quickly found out that the young man had noticed that we weren't there to collect admissions so he did it for us, and just as he finished telling us this, another Inuit fellow came up with some money. Eleanor thought he wanted to buy a picture, but Zebedee said, "No, no, he says there wasn't anyone there to take his admission, so he wants to pay now."

All smiles - Eleanor and Smilin' Johnnie.

Povungnituk honours us by singing Abide With Me

We could not believe our eyes and ears. We thought we came from a civilized part of the country but often we had difficulty getting people to attend our shows, and even then they tried to sneak past our doorman, or in through the exit door. Now these people that society, back then, in its ignorance, called "backward" and "uncivilized" were showing us a trait we wished our culture had more of - absolute honesty.

On this same evening, after the show, the people chatted briefly with their minister and he came to relay their message to us. They wanted to know if it was okay for them to sing a song for us. Eleanor, Guy and myself stood there with tears in our eyes as we watched and listened to about 350 sincere Inuit people sing, in their native language, *Abide With Me*. Later Mr. and Mrs Burroughs said that the people only sing that song for a very respected person who is leaving the community. They went on to say that we should feel very honoured as this was their way of showing their highest form of respect to a person or persons they love. I still have the tape recording of that song they sang for us. The parkas that Eleanor, Guy and I are wearing on our *Salute To Canada's Northland* LP cover were made at Povungnituk by those beautiful people. Oh yes, the third night, our gross was $368.

We were asked back to Povungnituk the following year, but the local priest Mr. Steinman, gave us a lot of opposition. He even placed an open letter in the press about our taking the bread and butter from the Inuit. We tried to get the local people's opinion on the matter by way of a petition okaying our visit. On our way to Povungnituk the next year, we met Mr. Burroughs in Moosonee. He was going to Toronto to see his wife who was in hospital, and he said he was very sorry he couldn't be there, but he hoped the Inuit would look after us.

When we arrived in POV it was unbelievable how these people met us. It was a glorious 'homecoming' and shortly after we landed we were escorted to the hall. Zebedee was about 15-years-old and was again our interpreter. He said the people of Povungnituk want you to use the hall to sleep in and eat in as well as hold your shows. We were to use the kitchen as our living quarters. As we were talking with Zebedee we noticed some fellows sawing a hole in the wall - a round hole. Then they brought some pipes and stuck them in the hole. Someone else brought a commode. After they assembled it, they stood looking at us, then at the commode, and laughed heartily. One fellow left and returned with some blankets that they put up around the commode for privacy - and they chuckled on. We had a little feast afterwards with canned food we had bought at the local store.

Smilin' Johnnie

We had many happy incidents like these with the Indian and Inuit people in the north which far outweighed the inconvenience of travelling the north country. Therefore, when we dedicated our *Salute to Canada's Northland* album to these folks, it wasn't to make a pot full of money, it was done with our sincerest, heartfelt thanks, admiration and compassion for these people who'd shown us such hospitality and love.

They accepted us as one of them.

At Cape Dorset (in August 1965) we landed with the Canso, but the tide was out and the beach was rocky. They came to get us from the plane with boats, but they had no place to dock the boats, so they carried us from the boat to the beach because we had no rubber boots.

The northern welcome was there, and nobody complained. Everybody was just too happy that we had come to greet them. We had supper with the RCMP officer and his wife, and stayed over with the people from the Hudson's Bay store. We were sorry that we couldn't spend more time at Cape Dorset, but we were lucky they held the aircraft overnight for us. We left early in the morning for Great Whale River, a community with four names: Whapmagoostui, to the Cree, Kuujjuarapik, to the Inuit, Poste-de-la-baleine, to the Quebecois and Great Whale River, to the English.

The people of Great Whale River must have realized the extra hardships that we went through to put on a show in these northern places - without a penny guaranteed for our services, or for the plane fare - because the crowds were good, and the people very appreciative. The weather was also with us on the trip, and the only settlement we couldn't make was Sugluk, but we kept it in mind for "next time." After about three-and-a-half weeks we were back home.

Smilin' Johnnie

SMILIN' JOHNNIE SHOW

After forty years ... the Smilin' Johnnie Show is still doing what they do best ... entertaining Canadians from coast to coast. Their brand of good clean country fun has had people laughing in the aisles, and clapping their hands to the tunes they fondly remember.

* **8** LONG PLAYING RECORD ALBUMS*
* **20** FULL LENGTH MUSIC CASSETTES*

Quality Entertainment At A Price You Can AFFORD

GOOD FUN GREAT MUSIC

Haven't you put it off long enough. Throughout the years, the Smilin' Johnnie Show remains a favorite. Remember ... big or small they play them all. For top of the line entertainment contact them today!

THE SMILIN' JOHNNIE SHOW

BOX 190-210 WROXTON, SASK. SOA 4SO

*The Biggest Little Show In Canada

Smilin' Johnnie's 40th anniversary promotion piece

31

21-GUN SALUTE AT SUGLUK

We'd been in the James Bay area several times, and every time we would add a settlement or two to our list. By this time we'd been as far north as Cape Dorset, on Baffin Island, a settlement of about 500 people, mostly Inuit, nestled in a few beautiful and colourful small rocky mountains just north of Hudson Strait. The Cape Dorset people were typical, friendly, Inuit people. They were continually asking us why we didn't go to Sugluk, just down the northern Quebec coast of Hudson Bay.

After hearing this for a couple of trips, I decided to go to see what Sugluk was like. I sent out the usual letters to the community and found out that there was a Roman Catholic mission hall that would be made available to us. The population of Sugluk was between 250 to 350 people. There was only one catch, the scheduled flights only landed every three days or so. This meant we'd have to stay over two nights to catch the next flight out. I remember we had landed there briefly one year on our way to another job in the north and the people had come aboard the plane to ask us if we could stop at their settlement.

When we landed at Sugluk, the usual northern Inuit welcome was there, not only the Inuit, but the white people were very friendly too. Quickly, someone directed us to a house that would be ours while we were there and the church

21-gun salute at Sugluk

brother offered us the use of the mission hall.

That evening the hall was filled to capacity. After the show, we visited with the brother, who was interested in electrical things and operated a ham radio station.

The next day, we were invited to a French family's home for dinner and they gave us Arctic char to take 'home' for supper. The second night we also had a full house, yet our gate receipts for the two nights just about matched the airfare to bring us in. However, money was not always the object and in these northern settlements, it seemed a shame to leave someone out when you were so close. Besides, I reasoned, I'd likely make it up somewhere else along the line.

The following morning we were waiting for the plane that was late as usual, when Lawrence Bourgeois brought over a young Inuit, about 20, to see me. He asked if it would be okay for them to shoot at me. I'd heard unusual requests, but this one topped them all. I asked him to repeat that, again he asked if they could shoot at us!

Just then someone came along as I was telling the young lad to do whatever he thought best! The other fellow explained that they wanted to give us a 21-gun salute.

I think I was more surprised at this than I was when he asked if they could shoot at us. I thought, 'Who are we, we're not dignitaries.' However, I certainly didn't want the people to think that we weren't honoured. So I told them they were welcome to do this if they wished. Afterwards the brother said he didn't know where they managed to find 21 guns in the settlement!

In due time the Canso arrived and we were hustled into the canoes (someone had taken the spark plug out of one of the motors, hoping to keep us in Sugluk!) and as we were taken to the plane, the Inuit men of Sugluk fired their guns and gave us a 21-gun salute. No royalty has ever felt more honoured or esteemed than our humble little show group that day.

As the twenty-first gun fired you could still hear the people cheering across the water.

As we boarded the aircraft, we looked at each other, Eleanor, Lawrence and myself. No eyes were dry. We didn't think we had done anything out of the ordinary. It was all in a day's work, but these dear people were grateful, and honoured us in this unique way. The pilot wanted to know what all the commotion was about and we said, through our tears, "They gave us a 21-gun salute!" I'm not sure he believed us, but pilots in the north country are used to unusual happenings!

It is not possible to mention every northern settlement, but this is an example of the way we were treated in most northern communities - except the people of Sugluk had a little more imagination. Usually a crowd just gathered, cheered, cried and waved as we left!

We didn't go to these communities to make money. That was a happy consequence, sometimes. We went because we knew these people had waited patiently for someone to come and entertain them. We also knew that no other groups were bothering to go. Believe me, once you've experienced the love and respect of these people it's not easy to forget.

I'll never forget them. They accepted us as one of them and we grew to feel honoured that they felt this way about us. In some cases I think we grew to know these people better than the welfare and government people who were charged with their wellbeing. Sure we made money in some settlements, but we also lost money in many more. I recall going to Nelson House, Manitoba - a chartered flight from Thompson - three times and not getting a crowd at any time. This isn't the only settlement where we didn't get an audience.

Actually, I think the reason the people of northern Canada took to us was because they realized that we weren't just coming to their community to make money, but to bring them the same kind of entertainment people in the more populated areas of Canada had enjoyed for years.

I'll grant you that the first venture I made into the north was with the idea of making money, but the people of the north changed that. As we made more trips north, I became more involved with their problems and felt compassion for these great people who welcomed us with open arms.

One of Smilin' Johnnie's early posters from the late 1940s

32

WE SURPRISE FROBISHER BAY
BY GETTING OFF THE PLANE SOBER

In September we did three weeks in British Columbia, but this province was not as good as even the prairies. It hadn't been in the '50s and it hadn't improved in the '60s. The only gain we made on that trip was the money we saved buying fruit. But we didn't buy much because we weren't making any money!

One day in November, I got a phone call from Frobisher Bay (now Iqaluit, the capital of Nunavat), on Baffin Island in NWT. We had been corresponding with them and were thinking of going there, but did not get any encouraging answers. This phone call was a pleasant surprise. It was a representative of three clubs in Frobisher Bay and he offered us $1,000 plus all our expenses while in Frobisher Bay, and one-way plane fare, for three nights entertainment. On our way back, he said we could play Fort Chimo, Quebec, which would help with our return fare and this would bring us back to Montreal. We accepted his offer and sent out our advertising.

We left Saskatoon on a Monday night and drove continuously, only stopping to fill the gas tank and our stomachs, arriving in Montreal on Wednesday night. Thursday morning we flew to Frobisher Bay. When we arrived at Frobisher, we were met by Gordon Rennie, the Hudson's Bay manager from Apex Hill, the Inuit settlement. He quickly took us to the hall with our instruments. We were a bit late so there was no time to let the instruments thaw out – condensation dripped off the accordion when we played.

157

We surprise Frobisher Bay

It was the usual northern welcome – wall-to-wall people with friendly smiles and chuckles. We had a very enthusiastic audience that night. The next night we were to have our show at the Federal Building where many entertainers the calibre of Bob Hope had entertained U.S. Air Force personnel.

We had a show and dance in this fabulous building, but the turnout wasn't as large as at Apex and it was somewhat subdued. The next night we were at Apex Hill again.

While in Frobisher Bay, we found out that there were entertainers from the U.S. as well as from Montreal and Toronto, and some CBC artists who had entertained there, but some of them came stumbling off the plane under the influence of liquor and some had made degrading and improper remarks about the place or the people.

The way these few entertainers had carried on, reflected on the other entertainers that followed. The people at Frobisher were quite surprised when we came in sober, cheerful, and did the job, especially when we were not nationally-known entertainers. From their descriptions, some of the biggest "pigs" were the real "big" entertainers from the U.S. and CBC. I guess they were surprised when "little" entertainers like us, with no big name to protect were the ones who behaved the best. It has always amazed me to hear that some really "big" names in the entertainment business are alcoholics or dope-addicts. I find this hard to understand because I've been in entertainment all my life and haven't found it necessary to resort to any of that. Sure we had drinks, but not to the point that we became alcoholics. We found the show demanded complete concentration and booze just blew that away. I think I've had just as many problems as anyone else - perhaps more than many. It seems to me, if I had what the "big" fellows had, I wouldn't need any other "lift" I'd be flying high without it.

I might mention that rooms were $25 per day at Frobisher and meals $4 each. Everything was in the Federal Building, the rooms, cafeteria, radio station, hall, bar, all the administrative offices. So many of the government people didn't even have to go outdoors during the winter if they didn't want to.

The accommodations were very nice and comfortable and the meals were absolutely terrific, but still we heard much complaining. We also found after getting to Frobisher that seven clubs had been approached to sponsor our show, but only three okayed it. The other four felt we were inferior because they hadn't heard of us. After they'd seen and heard us, they phoned and wanted to hire us at their clubs, but we didn't think this would be fair to those

Smilin' Johnnie

clubs who were footing the bills. We turned them down.

On the next scheduled flight south, we went to Fort Chimo. Once again the settlement was small, but the reception was big. We played there two days, and financially we didn't gain much except our plane fare back to Montreal, plus a couple of hundred dollars. At Fort Chimo we met Mr. and Mrs. Bob May who operated a tourist camp out of Chimo. They invited us to their house and we got to be real good friends!

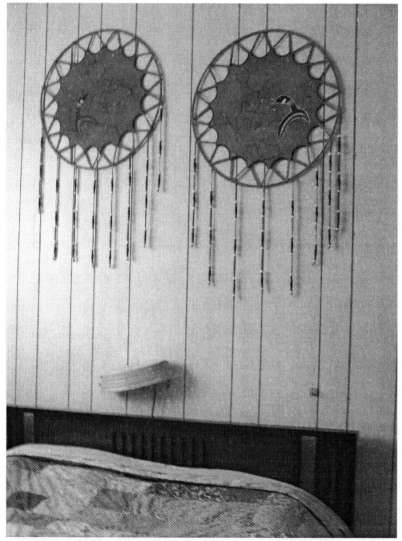

The dream catchers that hang over Smilin' Johnnie's bed are from Red Earth reserve, Saskatchewan, and the quilt is from Mistissini, a Cree community in Quebec.

33

ON THE GO FROM 9A.M. TO 5 A.M.
SOON CATCHES UP TO YOU

As 1965 came to a close, we decided to try a few weeks in the Yorkton area, starting 1966 - my twentieth year in the business - back home where it all began. We had thought of going on CJGX radio for a show or two, but we got on CKOS-TV instead. Our first date was January 8th at the Corona Motor Hotel Auditorium; with all the TV, radio, and posters, and newspaper advertising, we cleared $33. I soon changed my mind and changed our intended schedule of two months to two weeks.

In order to receive some attention from CKOS-TV, we offered to buy some spots announcing our dates, in exchange for 'free' live appearances on TV. After we had figured out the dollars we had to spend on our TV spots, the dollars we spent on newspaper ads, posters, plus telephone calls, car expense, we found ourselves going in the red. This was my first experience with TV people, but it sure didn't take us long to add the figures.

However, after talking to a few people in the TV market, many suggested that the cold weather in January was against us, and to give it more of a chance for publicity. So I changed my mind and stayed on CKOS-TV another four weeks. This was all of February. It was a lot of work for a very small reward. We would get up around 9 a.m., have breakfast, go to the TV station, get our instruments and costumes, set-up, tune-up, and dress up for the noon until 1 p.m. show. Then we tore down, packed everything in the cases, into the wagon, by this time it was about 2 p.m. and motored to our destination which would be anywhere from 75 to 150 miles from Yorkton.

We'd usually arrive just in time to set-up, tune-up, dress up, and play the show. After the show, about 11 p.m., we'd tear down, pack up, get into the wagon and head back to Yorkton. We'd arrive home anywhere from 3 a.m. to 5 a.m., have a bite to eat, get to sleep, so we could start the whole procedure again later that morning. This daily routine soon catches up with you.

During the month of February none of us had more than four or five hours of sleep a day. We travelled an average of 300 miles per day, yet our largest take for one show during that whole month was $161. When we left CKOS-TV we had a bill of over $300 which we were unable to pay because crowds had been so small.

Through correspondence and meeting once or twice, we knew Mr. and Mrs. Fabian Selois at Dawson City, Yukon. They, on occasion, had asked us to play at their tavern. I wasn't too impressed with bar work, so I had refused. However, this time, I thought I'd give it a try.

Fabian wanted a six-month contract, which I definitely couldn't accept, but we did agree on a three-week try out. We played at Dawson City for three weeks in the month of June. Although I didn't particularly like the atmosphere I was working in, it was different. We were playing to almost the same people every night and towards the end of the evening (2 a.m. was when they shut down) we were faced with the same old drunks, swearing was more than just common place, the tavern or lounge would be filled with cigarette, cigar and pipe smoke so thick you could almost cut it with a knife and it got thicker as the evening wore on. Our stage was next to the men's room. It wasn't a real pleasant aroma. Our wages were small, our tips were small too - lots of people offered to buy us drinks, but when we refused (you can only drink so much and still work), these people would never think of giving us that money so maybe we could buy a sandwich or something else. All they thought about was drinks. This type of thing went on from day to day – to just one big drinking party.

The one thing I did enjoy was that the sun shone at that time of the year in Dawson City, for almost 24 hours a day - the land of the midnight sun - this was really wonderful to see. It was worth the discomfort of playing in the tavern. I might say that Mr. and Mrs. Selois were very nice to us, we just weren't a bar group, our shows were family-oriented and we just couldn't accustom ourselves to the different atmosphere.

Since we had a booking at Springside, Saskatchewan, on Friday, June 24th, we

On the go from 9 a.m. to 5 a.m.

CKOS-TV Yorkton announcer Jim Horning promotes one of Smilin' Johnnie's LPs. Guy Coderre and Eleanor are with Johnnie.

had to cut our Dawson City engagement on Tuesday, June 21st and start home. We had the wagon all loaded up, and at 3 a.m. Wednesday, we left Dawson City. I drove all the way, the only time I stopped was to refuel and get an hour's shut-eye while Eleanor and Guy would go to eat.

We arrived at Springside tired beyond words and only an hour or two before show time. We set up, and were ready to go on, when a group of drunks came into the hall. There was no sign of anyone else and we were in no mood to put up with them so without any discussion we tore down, packed up and headed another 50 miles to my folks place in Wroxton, for a good night's rest - tired, disgusted and just plain mad.

We'd pushed ourselves to the utter limit to arrive in time to put on a show, and this was the appreciation we got.

Smilin' Johnnie

The next month or two, we relaxed a bit just playing a few sports days, rodeos, stampedes, and fairs on the prairies and east-central Canada. While travelling through Yorkton several times, we stopped in to make payments on our bill with CKOS-TV, and we were approached about doing another stint there in good weather. After some discussion, we decided to give it a try in October and November of 1966. Our turn-outs were somewhat better, our spots were a bit cheaper, but our trips remained the same, as CKOS-T.V. has four channels covering perhaps one of the largest viewing areas in Canada.

After this deal with CKOS-TV, I thought I might try a similar deal with CFQC-TV in Saskatoon, then at least I'd be right at home. To my surprise (in a way), I couldn't even get to see the manager, let alone talk to him. I was rather disappointed, but I'd had these deals before, so I wrote him a letter stating our request, and suggested that they contact CKOS for a recommendation, if necessary.

In the meantime, we made a deal with CKRD-TV in Red Deer. We found the weather was favourable in Alberta, but the attendance for shows was very, very small. Almost every community we went to did not watch CKRD-TV, they watched Edmonton or Calgary stations. Those who did come to our shows were really wonderful and almost every evening we were invited out for lunch or supper after the show. But after three weeks of small crowds, we had to give up on the Red Deer area.

I came home one day, and had a note to call Ken Hutson at CFQC-TV. He offered us a similar deal to others we had had with 'free' air time where we sang four or five songs, advertised our show dates, and in return we bought a certain number of commercials at the regular price. We found CFQC-TV personnel very nice to work with, though they were a bit more commercial than CKOS-TV. Had it not been for the commitment of buying commercial time I would have gladly accepted both Yorkton and Saskatoon stations for a longer period of time, but our revenue was too uncertain to gamble more time than we did. The weather was uncertain as well, making it hard for us to make our commitments. Although the revenue in CFQC was larger, our commitment to the station was also larger.

163

Smilin' Johnnie and Eleanor in an early promotion shot

34

GRANTS FOR CLASSICAL MUSIC – NOT FOR SMILIN' JOHNNIE

Even though we spent a great deal of time in northern Canada, we still played a good many dates in the rest of the country. We didn't spend all our time in the isolated areas. Usually, we would go to a northern area for two or three weeks, then come home and play the prairies or southern Ontario for two or three months before we'd be off north again. At this time, we did a lot of corresponding with the federal government in Ottawa and provincial government in Regina about getting in on the grant to bring live entertainment to the isolated parts of our country, but the government wasn't really interested.

I still hadn't given up getting the government to make some laws to restrict the influx of American entertainment, but what was one voice? There were so few professional groups left, mainly just new ones struggling to establish themselves, so there weren't enough people making complaints to the government for the politicians to even care, let alone do anything.

We had made many trips to the north, at our own expense. Now I don't pride myself on charging the Indian and Inuit people double our prairie admission for our show, especially when a good number of them didn't even understand English. But, how else could I possibly take them live entertainment? Even at this admission price it was touch and go. Whether the people understood the language or not, they enjoyed the show, and it sure didn't take them long to catch on to comedy.

Grants for classical music

It was difficult for us because many people had not seen a car, or a train, or a cow, or a sheep. All northerners were familiar with were canoes, dog teams, airplanes. The things that were in their all-too-isolated world. Remember, there wasn't TV in these communities then.

But we did bring a smile to their faces and we did our best to entertain them. After meeting us and seeing how much the local people enjoyed our show, many of the Area Administrators suggested that we apply to the Territorial Government for the grant that was available to subsidize travel expense for entertainers coming into the north. But, we found that this grant had to be applied for by northern community clubs and the Indian and Inuit people who enjoyed our show so much weren't usually in charge of the community clubs. These clubs in the north were usually run by teachers, store managers, or the clergy. Many of these people didn't want entertainment coming in or if they did, they wanted opera, or some other type of entertainment that the local people didn't really enjoy. So why the grant?

The Overture Concerts from Vancouver - where did they entertain? Inuvik, Yellowknife, Hay River were the only communities that had the population centres to support them. While that would satisfy the larger communities, there was still no entertainment in the smaller places.

I am hard-pressed to understand overture concerts and the folks in the north had told us how they felt about classical music. I was quite outspoken to government officials, and even to some local white people at Yellowknife and Hay River. I told them, "You guys don't need any grant, I'm concerned about getting entertainment to little places like; Arctic Red River, Fort Norman, Chesterfield Inlet, etc. You can afford to pay for your own entertainment if you want it, and quit squandering the government's money."

I could never understand why the grant went to such large centres, when little places like Holman Island, Pelly Bay, Igloolik, Spence Bay, etc., were totally stuck without any entertainment except what they made for themselves. I made a few enemies, I suppose, but I felt that the government grant was for the Indian and Inuit people who resided permanently in the north, and not for the white people who came in and went out as the spirit moved them.

However, all my talking was in vain. We never did get one penny of that grant money. Many of the Indian and Inuit people weren't even aware that such a grant was available.

Finally, I told the government, "By the time you decide to pay travel expense for a country and western group to go to these places, I will have played them all without your assistance." I didn't get to all of the tiny, remote communities, but I got to a good many of them.

Travelling in the north, I saw many times, some government people come in on a large aircraft - chartered for them - with many empty seats. So again I wrote Ottawa, and said, "If you think we're exploiting the Indians and Inuit, you have lots of your officials flying around the north, put us on the same plane, pay our wages, and we'll be happy to go all over the north and put on free shows for the people. After all, this is all we're working for, just to earn our living."

I received a nice letter, thanking me for the suggestion, and complimenting me for our efforts to entertain the people of the north, but it was virtually impossible to work the kind of deal I suggested, because they had many other groups who would like to go. Quickly I answered them, and asked - "What other groups? In the past 17 or 18 years I haven't seen any other groups, except for a few guys that work during the day and are moonlighting on the weekends, and they're not free to travel anywhere, so what groups are you referring to?"

They replied suggesting that I write the CBC, as they are responsible for bringing entertainment to Canadians. So we (again) wrote the CBC, explaining from beginning to end, who we are, what we've done, what we are doing, and what we were seeking. I knew what the answer would be before I put the paper into the typewriter, but it went anyway. I received a nice reply from the CBC expressing their concern about entertainment in the north. They went on to say that before they could consider us, they would have to consider people like Don Messer, Gordie Tapp, Tommy Hunter and the like.

This is exactly what I'd expected. I thanked the CBC for taking time to reply, and I made them a challenge: "You don't have anyone on radio or TV who could equal our show (we'd been together three-piece for awhile and were now a real solid show) or even come close."

I went further to challenge them to bring any three of their country and western entertainers and let them do a two-hour show and a two-hour dance in the north. They ignored our challenge. I thought, 'What a shame' and repeated what I'd said before . . . by the time the CBC pried someone out from their nest in Montreal or Toronto we will have played all of the north.

Looking back this was more than 40 years ago, and we've found that we've covered most of the north once, and in some places we've been a half-dozen times.

Grants for classical music

The CBC has taken some of its entertainers to the north, but usually to the bigger centres, not the smaller communities we chose to play, where sometimes only a handful of people would be in the audience.

I would like to point out that I never intended to elevate myself or my group as being superior to anyone in Canada. We were the only ones who were willing to sacrifice our comfort, our own money, and time to play these northern places.

Travelling conditions in the north at that time weren't all that plush. I don't want you to think that we're complaining about the north. The people gave us the best they had to offer. But, many times we changed costumes in a place that was nearly as cold as outside. Many places we stayed without having a square meal for a week at a time. Many times the local Indian or Inuit people took us in, and I don't think that the CBC had anyone at that time who would have been willing to work that way.

This is why I felt that we deserved the first chance at any subsidy which might be offered. We didn't want this only for ourselves, we also wanted to bring to the attention of the government and the CBC the need for good, clean, wholesome entertainment by groups that would get out of their city cocoons and see how the rest of Canada lives.

All Canadians don't live in Toronto, Montreal, Winnipeg, Vancouver, etc., which is where most of the CBC groups go. Don't kid yourself - they go to these places because they have the facilities, and because they can ask a big price from the larger centres. What about those Canadians who live in smaller settlements throughout our Canada? Don't these people also need live entertainment, or must they travel to the city for it? I'm not really blaming the CBC entertainers, because they are hampered by the dictates of the union, and by the fact that one gets awfully lazy and content playing to huge city audiences. They think there is no glory in playing to 200 people, even though those 200 might be the entire population of a town. Actually, a good many CBC entertainers just sit there and guard their throne so no one can take it away or push them off. They are quite content to stay in the city.

To the public this is nothing more than a welfare case and the CBC becomes a form of welfare to these people. It's soft, it's all in the studio, so why chase all over the country to entertain your fellow Canadians? Why indeed? Then I wonder why the CBC claims to bring entertainment to Canadians?

168

Smilin' Johnnie

Smilin' Johnnie and Eleanor display the brightly decorated guitar that shines under the black light they use at the end of their show. Created with tiny strips of coloured paper, the guitar recognizes Smilin' Johnnie's 60th anniversary on the road.

35

NEW YORK UNION STOPS APPEARANCE ON CBC'S DON MESSER SHOW

O ne day as our show on CFQC-TV was over, there was a phone call for me. This was nothing unusual, but when I lifted the receiver, I heard a man say, "This is Bill Langstroth calling from Halifax." At first I thought it was some local guys playing a joke on me. I knew who Mr. Langstroth was from having watched the Don Messer Show the odd time. He was the producer.

Mr. Langstroth went on to say that Don Messer was planning on a new idea for his show. Because it was Canada's Centennial year (1967), he wanted one singer or musician each week to represent each of the provinces. CBC in Winnipeg had suggested they use me as the singer to represent Saskatchewan. It seemed he knew more about me than I did.

Then he asked me if I would like to come to Halifax to be a guest on the Don Messer Show. I said that I would like to have my whole group, but he said their budget would only allow for one person. I said I would ask Eleanor and Guy what they thought, because I would have to cancel some dates.

I also informed Mr. Langstroth that I was not a member of the American Federation of Musicians (union), but he said that it would be okay. I would be able to work with an ACTRA contract. After some discussion with Eleanor, Guy and some of the staff at CFQC-TV, I called Mr. Langstroth and confirmed that I would be happy to appear on the show. Eleanor and Guy said they would do the TV shows alone and the country dates would be postponed. Mr.

Smilin' Johnnie

Johnnie finding it hard to smile these days

Smilin' Johnnie made headlines when an American union wouldn't let him sing on a CBC show.

Langstroth had given me details as to the arrangements, and what I was to sing - one song of my choice and a hymn. They would pay my return fare and hotel while in Halifax, so that was settled. This gave me only a day or two to make a few changes and cancellations in the Saskatoon area, and on our next TV show, we started making these announcements and changes. We explained to our viewing audience the reason for the changes and that I felt it was only right to accept the CBC proposition as a Canadian. Most of the viewing audience knew beforehand where I was going.

The next day, I left for Halifax, the hymn music was handed to me when I boarded the plane. I had about 10 hours to learn it while on board. We stopped at Winnipeg, I phoned some of my friends about the trip and told them to watch the March 6th show. I did the same when we stopped in Toronto.

About 11:30 p.m. I arrived at the Dresden Arms Hotel in Halifax. I phoned Mr. Langstroth, but he wasn't at the studio, so I phoned his home. He wasn't home, so I left a message for him to call me. A few minutes later, he called and said, "I had a b____ of a day today, fighting with New York. They must really have it in for you. New York said that if the CBC camera goes on you, they (the union) will put a freeze on the entire Messer group."

And then he said, "It would be stupid just to have you on camera to ask you how things are in Saskatchewan." Apparently the union secretary or president in Saskatoon had called union headquarters in New York and said that I was a problem to them. After listening to Mr. Langstroth, I said, "Well, what has New York got to do with our Canadian Centennial Show, they're foreigners aren't they?" Mr. Langstroth replied, "Johnnie, I only wish I could tell you."

I thanked him. I had sort of expected something like this to happen. Mr. Langstroth then mentioned that there were gale warnings which meant that flights west might be held up. He suggested that I take the next flight back to Saskatchewan, rather than wait and watch the rehearsal and meet the members of the cast.

New York union stops appearance on Don Messer

After this conversation with Mr. Langstroth I phoned home and explained all that happened. I told them to get on the typewriters and make a hundred copies of a letter to all the newspapers. By the time I arrived home, these were done and mailed. When Guy came to the plane to meet me, it was like a funeral. We were all very disappointed. I had a lot of sympathizers and they felt perhaps worse than I did.

The people at CFQC-TV weren't too happy either, but it seemed everyone was scared to say anything, scared to rock the boat. The next morning as I woke up, ready to go to CFQC-TV, I got a phone call to look at the Star-Phoenix before

---

NOTICE PAPER

No. 2,680—*Mr. McIntosh*—February 27

1. Was an invitation extended by telephone on February 8 by the C.B.C. to Mr. John M. Lucky of Saskatoon, to appear on a C.B.C. television show in Halifax representing Saskatchewan in a Centennial series?

2. Was he informed on arrival in Halifax on February 15 that he would not be able to appear because of objections by the American Federation of Musicians, New York office and, if so, what form did these objections take, and why were they allowed by the C.B.C. to influence their decision with regard to a scheduled appearance on a C.B.C. television show?

Notice of questions raised in Parliament in Ottawa when Smilin' Johnnie was not allowed to take part in a Don Messer Show marking Canada's Centennial.

I left. Sure enough, there on the third page, in bold type, "Johnnie is finding it hard to smile" and the letter which was sent to the editor was printed there in its entirety. They had gone one step further and questioned the local union representative as to why should it be an American Federation of Musicians - and not a Canadian union - the reply from him was "no comment."

It was obvious that the union men were in the dark. He was. After all, just a common laborer moonlighting as a musician on weekends. These union musicians didn't have the intestinal fortitude to go out and play full-time, yet were jealous of people who did. Somehow or other, they got to be union musicians with the dictatorship in their hands, yet they didn't even have the faintest idea how to operate a musical group full-time. All these people did was play weekends to pick up some beer money, and tax free cash income. As for musicians, we were the only group in Saskatoon available full-time. The rest were what many would class as sissies, or pansies, who were so filled with greed and jealousy that they envied the bare living we were eking out! They denied us the privilege of national coverage on one show for five minutes.

I asked myself many, many questions at that time. But above all, I thought to myself, 'This is our Canadian Centennial year - in the first 100 years our own Canadian brothers are ready to take the bread and butter out of our mouths. What will it be like in the next 100 years?'

I wondered 'are we celebrating Canada's Centennial with our hearts, or just because 100 years have elapsed?' I certainly couldn't see any unity, so what's to celebrate?

We wrote letters about this incident to all levels of government. The replies we received all said we had to be in the union. It was obvious to see that no-one was really interested.

The question was even brought up in parliament - why couldn't Smilin' Johnnie sing on CBC? The answer was because I wasn't in the union. No-one in Ottawa or elsewhere answered my questions as I had laid them out. What I really wanted to know was: Why had the Canadian government allowed the American Federation of Musicians dictate to the Canadian Broadcasting Corporation what it could broadcast and what it couldn't?

If we are so much under the American thumb, then why not just give up, and forget we're Canadians. What's the big deal with the Centennial? I was amazed at the big stack of replies I received from Ottawa and Regina, a briefcase full of everything but a simple answer.

Saskatchewan Premier Ross Thatcher was as close or closer than any. He said that the union question was a deep-rooted problem and one that the federal government would have to deal with because it was too big for the provincial government to handle.

Meanwhile, the federal government slumbered on while the unions it seemed, were conniving every conceivable means to ruin the country by grabbing, by getting and not giving, and it made me think of John F. Kennedy's words 'Ask not what your country can do for you, but what can you do for your country?' As those words rang in my ears, I could not help but get tears in my eyes, knowing that at the rate we Canadians were neglecting our country, in a few short years we might not even have a country.

From Model T to dog team

Two of the eight vehicles - many of them with more than 500,000 miles on them - that are parked on the Smilin' Johnnie homestead *Eight Miles North and One Mile East of Wroxton.*

36

FROM MODEL T TO DOG TEAM

We have travelled in practically every kind of transportation you can imagine. Cars, trucks, vans, taxis, buses, funeral home limos, gas trucks, boats, canoes, ferries, water taxis, freighter canoes, airplanes of all sizes from tiny Cessnas through to jumbo jets.

Travelling the Great White North we have been in the Bombardiers (snow-tracker people movers) and on individual snowmobiles. And, when you travel like we do, you make no special requests for transportation. We use whatever our hosts use – and when you are up in the Arctic, one of the most reliable ways of getting around is by dog team. We were never pulled by a dog team, but our equipment was often placed on a sleigh behind the huskies and taken from the airstrip to the hall.

It's special opportunities like this, seeing these dog teams at work, that have given Eleanor and me memories to last a lifetime.

Not every Canadian gets to ride with a team of huskies, even though this is a sort of icon image of Canada for many people throughout the world. Oh, I know many people think that folks get around Toronto in winter by dog team, but it is just the Inuit people today who use them as day-to-day transportation. And even then it is usually just those who still live the traditional lifestyle. The snowmobile is the preferred mode of travel for most of the people who live in the North, especially the younger ones, who like young people the world over, go for the speed and comfort and even luxury that goes with motorized

From Model T to dog team

The Smilin' Johnnie limo was held up by a rock-slide near Endako in northern B.C. on the way to a show in Prince Rupert.

transportation. I also find the young people of today don't mind paying the high prices we pay for gasoline. And don't forget, that when we are paying $1 a litre in the southern, populated areas of this great country of ours, those who live in the remote areas are sometimes paying almost twice what we pay.

They don't complain because they are young and don't remember the time when gasoline was 15 or 20 cents a gallon, which would be about five cents a litre. We didn't start using litres as the main measurement for gasoline until the Trudeau era in the 1970s.

While the young people today don't complain because they are not aware of the old prices for gasoline, we tend to accept gasoline prices as a necessary evil in the cost of doing business.

When you travel as many miles as we do in a year, even the slightest change in the price of gasoline can impact drastically on the bottom line. But, you know, we have lived our lives and gone about our business in entertainment, not worrying so much about the bottom line, but making sure that we were putting on a show that people would like – hopefully enough to invite us back again.

It was our first priority to put on a good show and put a smile on the faces of the people who saw us. Driving was just a part of the job.

Smilin' Johnnie

Long before I knew I was going to spend a lifetime driving back and forth across the country, I learned to drive in my dad's Model T and then he bought the Model A.

During the war, automobiles were hard to get hold of. Few were being manufactured because many plants were involved in making machinery for the war effort. But we did meet a fellow who sold us a 1942 Chevy on the black market.

When 1946 came along, the war was over, so I traded it off for a Chev DeLuxe. This was special because it was the first time we had a vehicle painted with gold lettering on the side, 'Smilin' Johnnie and His Prairie Pals.'

My road trips had already begun, even though back then we were still staying pretty close to home, more often than not getting home every night after a job.

I bought a 1949 Chrysler limo. I needed to get in five people and all the instruments. If heads turned when they saw the Chevy all painted up they really snapped to attention when they saw the limo.

My first and only Cadillac was a 1955 with just a few miles on it and an extended warranty. Six months later the engine started to fail. The extended warranty was not transferable from the seller to the buyer. I had paid $500 and took over payments, so I gave it back to them at GM in Yorkton.

I was doing about 100,000 miles a year. The roads were not as good as they are today so you had to trade off cars a lot quicker.

One of the most reliable vehicles I ever had was a 1953 Dodge I purchased after we moved to Regina following our stay in Swift Current where we had a half-hour radio show on CKSW.

I didn't like the Dodge, but it was so reliable. It would not wear out. It kept on going and going.

Only occasionally would I be without a car. And when that happened, for whatever reason, Dad usually let me borrow his vehicle.

The only prolonged time we were without a car was North Battleford and we didn't have enough cash to get one. We lived about two miles from the radio station and we walked there every day, No matter whether it was rain, sleet or snow, or bitterly cold, no one ever stopped to pick us up on the way to the radio station. No one ever offered to meet us at home and take us to the station, either. I could never figure that out. It wasn't the friendliest of places, but the radio station

From Model T to dog team

Winter roads are fine - in the winter. When spring arrives they tend to be more like streams. With Smilin' Johnnie on this trip from Hudson Bay, Saskatchewan to Mafeking, Manitoba, are Victor Pasowisty, Ray Lazar and Vickie Janescu. The car is the 1946 Chev with all the bells and whistles that cost $1,850.

was very kind to us. To travel to our jobs we borrowed cars or hired someone to drive us.

When we bought a 1964 Country Squire demonstrator it made heads turn. It was a beautiful vehicle. One day we smelled smoke and the vehicle burned. I had enough presence of mind to turn down the electric rear window so we could get the equipment out before the car burned. But there was no saving the vehicle.

We replaced the burned out vehicle with a 1965 Squire because the insurance company thought we had burned the 1964 on purpose. I like the Country Squire. It was ideal for us.

In 1969, Archie Couture, who was a dealer in Redvers said he could get us a really good deal if we got a Colony Park. It was always a special order with two reclining seats in the front and an extra gas tank.

Another little excitement was in a new Colony Park. We loaded all our stuff and we were driving along near Wynyard, Sask., when one of the band members said "Look, there's our wheel," and it was travelling along on its own speeding away from the car. I managed to keep the car from rolling and we came to stop and were able to get the vehicle fixed.

I traded the wagons between 175,000 and 200,000 miles. Had I known then what I know now I would have traded them every 400,000 miles.

I got a 1973 Colony Park and traded in the 1969 and two years later the person who bought the 1969 was still making 500 miles before adding any oil.

Colony Park wagons became our workhorse. They could fit us all in comfortably, plus all the instruments, including that human-sized bass fiddle.

178

Smilin' Johnnie

Guy Coderre, Eleanor and Smilin' Johnnie take a breather in North Battleford in 1964 with the Ford Country Squire that later burned.

And after a while I started running the Colony Park to the max. Or pretty close to their limit.

In fact, after we had 400,000 or 500,000 miles on a Colony Park we just stopped using it for everyday trips to shows and bought a new one. The trade-in price was so minimal it was not worth trading it. The vehicles were still in running order and we decided to keep the vehicles in our yard for spare parts. After all, we have 40 acres, lots of room for spare parts.

We have eight pre-1979 Colony Parks' on our property at present. All have at least 500,000 miles on them. Four are next to drivable and four are in pieces.

Our yard is where Ford Mercury Colony Parks come to die. We don't do hundreds of thousands of miles any more, but we keep them just in case we need a spare part one day.

Maybe one year I will sell them on the Internet to people who like to restore these 460-horse-power beauties to all their original glory.

Colony Park, as I said, was a real workhorse. Ideal for what we needed. You could load them like a camel. We are really glad Archie Couture suggested them.

The reason we stopped buying the Colony Park was Ford started making them smaller and flimsier after 1978.

I wrote to Ford. I was looking to find a previous year model without any miles on it, but they couldn't find one anywhere in Canada. That gives you an idea of how popular they were and you would have thought that Ford would have done all the figuring to determine that this great vehicle they had would be worth preserving and continuing to produce, rather than downsizing and taking away some of its strengths.

However, in the letter telling me they couldn't find a Colony Park for me, they said that when I was next in Oakville I should stop by and they would buy me lunch. My mother said "Not even dinner. Just lunch." My Mom had a sense of humour, but she also was semi-serious when she made this statement, knowing how many Ford and Mercury vehicles we have purchased brand new over the years.

Neither was it the first time I had written to Ford. In fact, I told the story earlier of driving from Saskatchewan to Oakville – while I was on tour in Ontario – to talk to them about the fact North Battleford garage was not doing warranty work for us because we had bought the car in Winnipeg.

And on the way back from Ontario I was driving a Marquis Colony Park with 197,000 miles on it. I stopped at the Ford – Mercury dealer in Steinbach that was advertising "good deals" to see what my wagon was worth.

I went to make a telephone call and the salesman, without my permission, took my wagon for a test drive and under full throttle and with our 1,500 pounds of instruments and tapes and luggage loaded in the back, destroyed the motor in just a few minutes.

They then accused me of bringing the vehicle in for a trade knowing the engine was not working properly. They wouldn't believe me that I wasn't planning on trading the vehicle immediately. And the salesperson denied he had taken the car without my permission.

Our station wagon was useless and the garage didn't have a wagon on the lot. Another time we had problems in the dead of winter. It was New Year's Day,

Smilin' Johnnie

Eleanor works on the 60th anniversary costumes, wearing one of the tee-shirts she designed.

we had played New Year's Eve at Thompson until 3 a.m. and then we visited with friends until 6 a.m. before leaving for the next job

The car stopped and the red light came on about 20 miles out of town. This was a brand new car. We sat there for three hours. Of course, this was before the cell phone and the roadside assistance programs that are part of every new car deal today. We were starting to feel comfortable which means the body was beginning to think it could survive the extreme cold. It was 58-below zero and no time to give up, or to make silly decisions.

One of the band members, Guy Coderre wanted to get out and walk. But we stopped him. He would never have made it. When it is that cold, it only takes a few minutes for disaster to take over.

At about 10 a.m. a fellow came by on his way to check his cabin at the lake. He stopped to help us.

We've travelled all these millions of miles and escaped serious injury even though we have been involved in a few accidents.

There were a couple of vehicles we had that were written off in crashes, but we also escaped with scrapes and bruises. I had a big 1952 Buick Roadmaster with a straight 8 motor (longer than a v-8) and going up a steep incline it deprived the engine of oil and that was the end of the engine.

Another time, we were on our way home from a dental appointment in Dauphin, Manitoba.

We were following a grainliner at 65 mph. There was a wind warning, but the Dodge Spirit is a little different than driving the wagon.

The truck started slowing down. We thought he wanted me to go by, but as we got even with the truck he started crowding us. We had to take to the ditch. When we got to the bottom of the 25 or 30 feet ditch our car rolled onto its roof top.

People stopped to help. The car was totalled. We were upside down. I was okay but when I talked to Eleanor she did not reply. She was just hanging there in her seatbelt. Frantically, I shouted a couple of times, "Are you okay? Are you okay?" She didn't answer. I thought, ' oh no, not this way.' She was quiet because she was concentrating on trying to find the ignition switch to turn off the motor.

Eleanor was hanging upside down in her seatbelt. Her forehead was resting on the windshield.

I managed to crawl out.

The ambulance, police, paramedics were all there, but we didn't need them. Eleanor was freed and the seat belt had done its job and protected her. Oh, we were sore, but no broken bones and no hospital treatment needed. That's about as close as I'd ever want to come.

Smilin' Johnnie

Guy Coderre with Eleanor and Smilin' Johnnie

Best man stays on for honeymoon

Smilin' Johnnie and Eleanor on their wedding day with the best man, John Sigurdson, and his wife, Ethel.

37

BEST MAN STAYS ON FOR HONEYMOON!

When you work for yourself every time you take a holiday you don't get paid. So, when we were planning our honeymoon we decided to book five nights at a club at Naicam Station, about 100 miles east of Saskatoon. What we didn't plan was having the best man sleep in our room!

John Sigurdson, a member our church, dropped by to see our show one night, but a typical January storm blew in and he was unable to get back to Saskatoon.

During one of the intermissions of our show he went to get a room at the motel where we were staying. When they told him there were no vacancies he told them to put a cot in our room. His wife, who was not with him, was upset with him because he bunked in with us.

But we didn't mind.

When you travel as much as we do you are so thrilled when people put themselves out and make room for you. This was just one way to pay back all the hundreds of families that put themselves out to make us welcome in their homes . . . even though it was our honeymoon!

38

NO TWO COMMUNITIES ARE THE SAME

New Year's Eve we wound up 1969 at Wabowden, Manitoba and from there we played repeat engagements at Easterville, Cross Lake, Norway House, Oxford House, Island Lake, Ste. Theresa, Split Lake, Nelson House and many other inland isolated settlements. The only way to get to many of these settlements at that time, was by plane or snow machine.

Usually you charter, but if you're not really careful to arrange a split charter, you get stuck paying a double charter. These airlines are pretty handy with a pencil and paper! Once the aircraft drops you off at the Indian settlement, you are at the mercy of the local people which can be good or terrible depending upon the people.

There are extremes and no two settlements in the north are alike. Sometimes the people are waiting for you and take you and your equipment to the hall. But other occasions you have to carry your own equipment to the hall, only to find it is locked. Sometimes a local person picks you up with a snow machine or Bombardier and they often do this free of charge, sometimes they charge as high as $20 to go three miles. Back when we were first travelling into these northern communities – many of them remote outposts – there were no hotels, no cafes, no phones, only the odd two-way radio in many of these places.

You have to be prepared to live with the local people for as long as you're there. If the weather gets bad, you could be there a week or more - so you live on sardines, or salmon, bread (or if no bread is available, crackers), cokes, chocolate bars, etc.

In many settlements the local people will take you into their homes. In some cases they move out and give you the whole house, and in other cases just a room or a bed. The price varied from $3.50 per person to $20 per person back in the '60s and '70s. Now you can pay $150 or more a night to stay in a hotel/motel and $30 to $50 for a bed in a house or a trailer.

It's true that the people do come out and see the show in these places - about 30 per cent to 50 per cent of the population attends. But by the time you're finished paying for your accommodations and airfare, plus your car expenses back home, you hope you have enough left for a small wage.

In these northern settlements, you learn very quickly to have patience. If you didn't they'd take you out in a strait jacket. No-one hurries in the north. There's lots of time, you can't follow a certain pattern. Posters for certain dates and times, quite often mean nothing. Just before show time the chief and councillors may come along and say they've decided to hold a meeting.

You cannot argue, they are the authority, and besides, it could be 35-degrees below zero and the aircraft is not there. You're staying on their reserve, you accept their rules. I mentioned before that each northern settlement is different and usually a community won't remain the same two years in a row, so you're dealing with a people and a country that's in a constant change.

Lawrence Bougeois with Smilin' Johnnie and Eleanor.

No two communities are the same

In many cases, we found that the reason we had problems with some of the Indian chiefs and councillors, was because they were under the influence of some white people. Where the Indian people were left to make their own decisions they were usually fine to deal with.

In the early months of 1970, we were not making any far-reaching tours, usually this time of year was reserved for annual trips to northern settlements which were a little easier to reach during the winter months. These northern trips meant a lot more work for all of us, loading aircraft, arranging accommodation, making sure the equipment was in the right place at the right time and I began to notice Lawrence Bougeois, who had replaced another good worker and musician, Guy Coderre, was losing interest in his job.

Lawrence was only 15 when he joined us and I looked at this as an opportunity to help a young man get into the business, just as Mr. Tetoff did for me with his dance band.

Lawrence, who was a Metis from High Level, Alberta, did very well. He handled lead guitar and fiddle, and jumped into the comedy routine and was well liked by the audiences.

He was with us for three years. But unfortunately left us without reason and without notice to go back home. He left his clothes and his guitar. We were sorry he didn't say goodbye.

However, we were pleasantly surprised and gratified to get a letter from him in December 1993, 23 years after he left the group, telling us "I realize the education I received from our association, was totally unique. The kind of education that most people never have the opportunity to get. What a whirlwind three years that was! We did a lot, didn't we? Wow!

"I'll always be thankful for the patience and support you both gave to me so unselfishly during what must have been a challenging time! You truly are very special people . . . I know your moulds were destroyed!

"It has taken me a long time to realize what a great gift I received in those three years . . . crops take a long time to grow . . . the seeds you both planted then have grown and reproduced in abundance . . . thank you both."

In the three years he was with us, Lawrence had seen more of Canada than most people do in a lifetime, and he'd earned more money than most fellows his age. When he took the bus back to his folks it was a shock to us, and it hurt.

Smilin' Johnnie

...lin' Johnnie was all smiles when Moose Factory resident Daisy Turner, right, brought along ... of Johnnie's 1960s LP records to get his autograph at the 2004 Gathering of the Cree in ...se Factory. Johnnie signed the record which Daisy bought back in 1968. Also in the picture ...ohnnie's wife, Eleanor.

39

ELEANOR TAKES OUT DENTURES – JUST FOR LAUGHS!

When Lawrence moved on we were left with a dilemma – who's going to do the comedy act?

I decided I would put on the overalls and Eleanor was the 'straight man.'

It didn't go well. We had to make a change after only one show! Now, with only two of us, it meant that Eleanor and I would simply change roles – she would do the comedy. I would be the straight man.

And so, Olga the Janitor was born.

It was a raucous success right from the start.

What made it that way was Eleanor's decision to take out her dentures for the role of Olga.

For 30 years she has been taking her dentures out to make our audiences laugh. They love Olga.

It didn't have to be like that. It was Eleanor's idea to remove her dentures. But I sure appreciate her willingness to do what she does. She often says that if you ever have stage fright - or are shy on stage - doing comedy soon cures you of any jitters.

Smilin' Johnnie

It is a good, clean, family type of comedy, with a lot of groaners and one-liners. We have found the audience likes this type of humour.

For example, Olga says she likens being in love to being in a sewer. We banter back and forth and then she gives the reason for being in love and being in a sewer being the same . . . "you can get all messed up with either one," says Olga.

It's simple stuff. But it's fun. The comedy is a big part of our show. Our audiences love it and we love doing it.

Eleanor dressed - and with teeth parked - ready for the fun to begin.

40

The Laffin' Jack Rivers Show!

When I first started writing a book back in the early 1970s while living in Saskatoon I was contacted by a teacher at the University of Regina who did some work for CBC.

He asked us to let him know when we would be in Regina so he could video tape some segments and interview us for a television show.

We arranged for this to be done at our show in Avonlea in November 1972. The audience seemed a bit perplexed by all the extra lights and paraphernalia needed to do videotaping.

He ended up videotaping the entire show and besides interviewing us he also interviewed members of the audience.

A day or two later CBC-TV aired a five-minute program about us.

It was a good piece about us and I liked working with him, so I showed him a copy of the transcript of the book and asked him if he would be interested in helping me with it, after all he was an English teacher.

He was quite interested and said he would be glad to help, especially if I wasn't in hurry, because he was busy.

We sent him a copy of the manuscript and once in a while he would send us a card, but we never did get the manuscript back.

A few years went by and we moved to Wroxton. We didn't hear from him, but

Smilin' Johnnie

CKCK PRESENTS

Saskatoon's
25th Street Theatre Production

TONIGHT

THE LAFFIN' JACK RIVERS SHOW

Performing at
7 OAKS MOTOR INN
(formerly Holiday Inn)
777 Albert St.

SHOWTIME - 8:30 P.M.
Box Office 525-6686

A newspaper advertisement for The Laffin' Jack Rivers Show, supposedly based on the life of Smilin' Johnnie.

we knew he was busy writing plays because we heard them advertised on CBC radio.

One day I got a telephone call from my son, Jerry, who was manager of the CFMC-FM Stereo 103 radio in Saskatoon. He said the person with our manuscript had been into the station to see him about promoting his new play.

As they were discussing this play, the writer said that he had loosely based it on the life of a fellow called Smilin' Johnnie and he asked Jerry if he knew him.

"Of course, I do," said Jerry, "He's my dad."

Apparently, the writer then stuttered and murmured something like "I suppose he'll be suing me now."

The play was on stage in Saskatoon and Jerry used the complimentary tickets to take his brother Bob and his wife.

Throughout the play, I am told my daughter-in-law cried when she saw how they portrayed myself and Eleanor.

The Laffin' Jack Rivers show

They had us swearing. Eleanor was little more than a prostitute.

Jerry told me to get a lawyer and go to see the play when it came to Yorkton.

The play was called *The Laffin' Jack Rivers Show* and it was coming to Yorkton in a week or so.

Jerry sent me complimentary tickets and my lawyer and Eleanor and my mom went along to see the show. In that short time from when the show played in Saskatoon to the time that it played in Yorkton a lot of things were changed. There was still lots of foul language and many incidents we recognized from our manuscript, but nothing like my son said was in it in Saskatoon.

A friend and neighbour, Fred Perpeluk, was selling admission tickets for the play and I asked him on the way out how many people had attended. He said about 70, 30 of which were free passes.

The play was sponsored by the Arts Council. For years, I had been trying to get them to sponsor our show, but they never even answered me.

I had also enquired about renting the Anne Portnuff Theatre, where the play was held, but their price was a firm $350 per night.

I asked Fred who picked up the tab for the theatre rental and he said he didn't know, but he thought the Arts Council or the government.

Next day my lawyer called to say he was thoroughly disgusted with the show and said it was a waste of an evening, but he felt there was nothing worthwhile to go after.

It is sad what people will do to other people. We'd hear the promotion people interviewed on radio saying the play was based on some fellow who was on the skids and they'd play this up for all it is worth, even though it was a lie. No-one took time to check-out the so-called facts. When something is spoken on air you can't erase it, even though it is only gossip.

Not all of those who have interviewed us over the years have taken advantage of us like that particular writer did.

Wayne Rostad had us as guests on his Gemini award-winning television show, *On The Road Again*. And we will ever be grateful to Peter Gzowski, who included us on his *Morningside* radio program when he was in Regina.

It was an honour to be on both of these famous Canadian programs.

I was impressed with the interviewing abilities of Peter Gzowski. He had the ability to listen to what was being said by his guests and then following paths

Smilin' Johnnie

Smilin' Johnnie and Eleanor received this postcard from Peter Gzowski after appearing on his popular CBC *Morningside* radio show when it visited Regina.

that were created by the answers, rather than moving from one set question to the next. This often breaks the continuity of the interview, but Peter's fresh questions kept the story flowing and interesting. I remember he asked me where I had been playing shows in the last little while. Instead of mentioning a lot of the little towns we had been to, I said "I can tell you where I haven't been - to the O'Keefe Centre" (now the Hummingbird Centre in Toronto). He laughed at the answer and picked up right away, obviously thinking there was a lot of people and places to talk about all over the country.

As we had waited for the show to start, Peter was told by the producer that it was to be a 15 to 20-minute interview and that if necessary there was one of our recordings keyed and ready to go. The interview took the full time slot. In fact, I thought it could have gone on longer, such was the talent of Peter.

Wayne Rostad and his crew got to us through a huge blizzard, one of those 'storms of the century.' As part of the introduction to the interview they played part of a newscast from the previous day that said that all roads in the province of Saskatchewan were impassable and motorists should stay off them.

41

WE DON'T EAT BEFORE A SHOW

It wasn't that we were not hungry, nor were we not capable of playing on a full stomach . . . or superstitious that if we ate we'd maybe not be as sharp as we should on stage for our audience.

Simply, we often couldn't afford to eat.

Didn't matter where we were. We ran our lives and our show close to the bone. There was no credit back then and debit cards were decades away from helping to make life almost a cashless society.

We had to make sure that we had enough money to put gas in the car to get to the next job. Sometimes that meant we would have to buy gas rather than food.

We would get into town, set up the instruments to get ready for the show and then the organizers wanted to go out to eat. It was suppertime, after all. We just used the excuse "We don't eat before the show," and everyone respected that.

Sometimes we hadn't eaten all day. But we couldn't eat until we were paid. And we didn't get paid until after the show. Then we had to make sure we had enough gas to get to the next job.

I remember going into Chapleau, Ontario in late summer/early fall 1967. All three of us had pooled our last pennies to buy gas to get there.

Smilin' Johnnie

We, literally, did not have a cent between us. We didn't know what kind of an audience to expect. To our delight, it was a full house. And so Chapleau has always had a soft spot in our hearts. Not to mention the all-night café that came to help us battle the hunger pangs.

When we did have a few dollars we would accept the invitation of the local people to eat supper before the show, just to be sociable. We met a lot of people over supper and many of them became our friends. But we were always careful what we ate. It is not easy singing on a full stomach, you end up burping a lot and that's not good to hear over the microphone. And I know that Eleanor couldn't hold the accordion properly after a full meal, or she would get heartburn.

We always had a good time at the Le Goff reserve near Cold Lake, Alberta. So much so that they wanted us to come back to play when everyone was home.

They picked New Year's Day 1969.

Unfortunately, I wasn't feeling too well. I think the flu bug was getting the better of me. I know you are thinking that too much partying on New Year's Eve was the reason for the illness, But it wasn't. We got to town, set up a few hours before the show and I decided to take a rest at the hall while everything was quiet. I thought if I could get some sleep I would be better come show time.

I hadn't been asleep very long when one of the local men who was still celebrating the New Year - and letting the booze do the talking - came back stage. He got rude and obnoxious.

Some of the ladies of Le Goff came along and took him away but told us "That fellow is going to give you trouble all night, and there were many more like him outside, so we'll help you, you'd better just load up and leave."

And that was that. We got away without further incident. This was one of the very few times that anything even remotely near trouble happened.

Smilin' Johnnie

Smilin' Johnnie has always done all his own bookings and promotions. The office (above) has gathered many more posters, letters and mementoes since the early days (below).

42

WE DID ALL OUR OWN BOOKINGS

After the first trip to northern Canada every settlement would ask, 'Are you coming back again next year?' So it became an annual trek for us. Every March or April we went up the Mackenzie Highway to Yellowknife and north to the Delta (Mackenzie). And every summer we took the swing around James Bay and Hudson Bay. Of course, we still played dates on the prairies the rest of the year, but we felt sort of obligated to return each year to the northern settlements, as they had no other live shows. They looked forward to seeing us every year. Every once in a while we'd add a new settlement like Cambridge Bay, Coppermine or Holman Island, NWT, or Rainbow Lake, Alberta, which wasn't even there when we made out first trip up the Mackenzie Highway before the big oil boom.

I must stress, that these trips to northern Canada, especially the Delta, were very, very expensive and we risked losing a great deal of money. But we were still unable to get any assistance from the government. We just held our breath when we got on the aircraft to fly north—hoping that we'd make enough to pay our fare and have a little left over for wages. It was bad, because these northerner's supported the show to the hilt, but the cost of transportation was so high we didn't realize much profit.

Upon returning to Saskatchewan from a northern trip, we had stacks of mail - many letters from the Maritimes asking us to come back. So we booked May and part of June in the Maritimes, and included Newfoundland on this trip.

We did all our own bookings

We stopped to visit some of the folks we'd met the past fall and made some new friends too. It was our first trip to Newfoundland and we were all thrilled with the ferry ride over there, even Eleanor's dog Misty (acquired from Glen Speers the Hudson's Bay store manager at the Cree community Mistassini Post, now Mistissini, Quebec), enjoyed it.

Newfoundland was a new and exciting experience for us. We found the people friendly and humble. Some places we were invited out for supper or lunch as hospitality was offered with open arms. Now we could say we had covered all of Canada. Carbonear was the furthest east we went in Newfoundland, and we'd been out to the Queen Charlotte Islands and as far north as Holman Island, north of the 70th parallel, so we'd covered the country. We'd met Canadians from every corner of the country and counted them among our friends. We made it a habit to stop at the same truck stops and gas stations so we got to be friends with the people.

During 1969, we played the prairies, the Maritimes, Ontario, Quebec, the Yukon, NWT, and British Columbia. Always we did our own promotion, ticket selling, long-playing records, bookings, driving, unloading the wagon, setting up the equipment, keeping costumes cleaned and pressed, in fact everything to keep a band on the road 52 weeks a year. It was a lot for a three-piece group to do.

We didn't have a manager, a bookings agent, a PR person, roadies, stage hands. There was just the three of us – and we shared the extra duties that were all necessary to put us on stage and on time.

We averaged 100,000 miles by car yearly, but couldn't keep track of the miles we made by plane, boat, snow machine., train, and even dog team! When we made a booking, we made every effort to get to it! Also in October of 1969, we made a quick trip up to Cantung, NWT at the Canada Tungsten Mine, about 200 miles north of Watson Lake, Yukon, just across the NWT border. They gave us a lovely guest house and we found it a very interesting trip, and a very beautiful spot. In December of 1969 we made a return trip to Frobisher Bay and Fort Chimo.

43

BIGGEST PAY DAY USED TO DIG WELL

Our biggest payday in 60 years of travelling was when we opened for the RCMP Musical Ride in Grimshaw, Alberta.

It was 1987, and we were offered $8,500. We called our friends, Stew Clayton, the Singing Farmer at Darlingford, Manitoba, and asked him and his wife, Marge, who played the keyboard and sang with Stew, to join us.

They were delighted and we had a great time. We shared the $8,500 and used our portion to dig a well at our home. After all, we had been there for 10 years and had been hauling water in five-gallon pails all those years, except in the winter when we melted snow for water.

Stew and Marge were leaving early the next morning and asked if they could be paid cash instead of cheque. This was no problem for the organizers.

However, Eleanor had a bit of a scare walking back to the hall. They loaded her up with a purse full of $20 bills. On the way to take the money to Clayton a truck pulled up alongside. She felt that she was going to be robbed. Instead, the driver gave her a home-made cassette tape and suggested it was a song that he thought we should play.

When you play the kind of music we play, you have to have the right kind of audience.

Biggest pay day used to dig well

In the 80s we started contacting seniors clubs across the country. And, sure enough, many were wanting the kind of entertainment that we provided.

I think our show takes them back in time and brings out all sorts of memories for the seniors.

One thing about seniors club appearances is that you don't have the hectic three shows a day schedule. In fact, many of the shows are in the afternoon, so there are no late-nights. In fact, seniors are not too interested in evening shows.

However, just last year, in 2005, we were asked to put on our show at two nursing homes in Selkirk, Manitoba. A friend asked us to split the three-hour show in two and put on two 90-minute shows – one at each nursing home. We agreed. But that's easier said than done.

A lot of equipment has to be hauled from the station wagon to the hall and then back out again to the station wagon and then out of the wagon again to the new hall.

There was some little thing that we hadn't counted on . . . it poured rain all the time so we were drenched several times that day.

44

MISTY THE SINGING DOG

My story would not be complete without a chapter devoted to Eleanor's dog, Misty, a beagle. After all, Misty was devoted to us.

Misty was part of the family for more than a dozen years. She was given to us on one of our trips into the Cree community of Mistissini, Quebec.

Misty always appeared on stage with us, but was quiet and exceptionally well-behaved. You can imagine having a dog on stage with you for three hours and her just lying there – happy to be close by, but not seeking, let alone demanding, any attention.

Then one day at home, lying on the chesterfield, she started to 'sing' when we were playing *How Great Thou Art*.

The more we tried to quiet her, the louder she got.

We always closed with this hymn, or *Just A Closer Walk With Thee*, and Misty quickly became a part of the closing number.

We didn't encourage it. Didn't have to. As soon as the music started, Misty began her singing.

The crowd always loved it. And obviously Misty loved it too. Maybe it was something to do with it being the end of the show and she knew that we would soon be giving her attention, happy to think that she would soon be on

Misty the singing dog

Eleanor's lap for the ride to the next job – usually a long car ride - and she would be close to us for hours on end. Misty loved the comfort of sitting with Eleanor. She was happy just to be close. Misty didn't need constant attention. In fact, Eleanor was even able to do a lot of needlepoint and crochetting while travelling in the car.

Whatever it was, Misty never missed a beat. As soon as that music started, Misty sprang to her feet and started doing her thing.

We didn't encourage the singing, but there was nothing we could do to stop it. There was no training, no rehearsal. Just a dog singing to her heart's content. Happy with her life. But in Austin, Manitoba, they tried to say we needed a government license to operate a trained animal show. We never trained her. She was a natural. We never did buy a license and it was never suggested again by anyone in government.

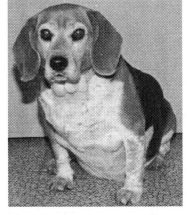

For 12 years she was as much a part of the show as we were. She never let us down. The audience used to love Misty and she used to love the candy, the pop and the chips that she was given by her fans at the end of the show.

One day at home she went missing. Remember, we have 40 acres, so it is easy to lose your way. Eleanor went inside and played *How Great Thou Art* on the tape player and then turned it up so it could be heard outside. It wasn't long before Misty strolled back to the house.

Misty travelled everywhere with us. I don't think it was easy for her. She went all over the country with us. Didn't particularly like the noisy airplane rides, and never really enjoyed the rough roads and the Bombardier rides. She just clung to Eleanor. I think it was the noise that she didn't like.

One airplane ride she was doing her usual squirming as we were climbing into a Beaver. I didn't have a good grip on her and she slipped out of my arms and into the water. I quickly scooped her up by the tail when she bobbed up and before she had a chance to drift away from the dock. After that, when you picked her up to load her onto a plane she didn't move.

She died Feb. 26, 1979, after a brief illness, at precisely 8 p.m. – the time we usually started our show. We miss her. We have never replaced her - we can't. She is irreplaceable.

Smilin' Johnnie and Eleanor relaxing in their living room, surrounded by plants and mementoes from their hundreds of trips across Canada.

45

'FRIENDLY REUNIONS' AT HOME

When we were home we had a lot of friends stop by. Many of them suggested that our lovely yard would make a great place to hold a jamboree.

In the late 80s we wrote to friends and invited them to a "friendly reunion."

We had so many positive replies that we scheduled two Jamborees – one the second weekend of July 1988 and the other the third weekend of August.

If we thought travelling and playing shows was a lot of work, staging these jamborees was a whole lot more work.

Without a riding lawn-mower, just mowing the grass was a two-day job.

Then there was a stage to build, as well as a food booth to be erected and a place to sell our cassettes.

I didn't have any experience in carpentry, but managed to build the stage and it stood for all the years of the jamboree. In fact, it is still standing today.

Friends donated outdoor toilets and Paul and Eddie Achtemichuk pitched in to help with many things, including a lot we hadn't anticipated.

That first year the whole family got involved with the jamboree. Jerry, the eldest son, who was living in Edmonton, came to emcee, and second son, Bob, came from Saskatoon to sell tickets at the gate.

Smilin' Johnnie

Aerial view of the Lucky homestead *Eight Miles North and One Mile East of Wroxton* at jamboree time. The house, garage and greenhouse are on the left, the stage is in the middle and the food booth is just to the right of the stage. Cassettes were sold by the entertainers in the booth to the left of the stage.

Mom Lucki sang a Ukrainian song with Johnnie and was a big hit – even with those who didn't understand Ukrainian.

Some friends helped with the food booth and the cassette booth. Plus we had invited a lot of our entertainer friends to perform.

The first year everyone danced on the grass, but in subsequent years we built a dance floor over the grass in front of the stage.

We learned a lot the first year. We decided that we would have only one jamboree a year – two was just too much work.

However, the next year we had three!

We usually served all the entertainers chili in the house at the end of weekend and another tradition was the authentic Saskatchewan food, Wheat Salad, which was a favourite, particularly with the out-of-province musicians.

They loved it. Everyone loves it. You boil the wheat and then when it has cooled, blend in pineapple, cream cheese and Dream Whip. It doesn't last long, no matter how much you make.

We always tried to be home a week or two before the jamborees – which ran

'Friendly reunions' at home

Smilin' Johnnie and his wife, Eleanor, with his Mom, Mary, singing at the jamboree.

for a decade. We needed to repaint the toilets and some of the other outdoor buildings, just to freshen them up.

The Doukhobor choir from Kamsack regularly performed at our jamboree. We were honoured to have them come along. They did such a wonderful job. There were 10 or 12 choir members and they sang in Russian. It was very moving. Very good.

The 1996 jamboree was a special one – it celebrated my 50 years in the music business. A special visitor was Lawrence Bourgeouis, who played with us in the 1970s. A couple from North Battleford sang a very nice song they had written for us and our dear friend Lawrence Zelionka wrote a poem, which he read from the stage. He presented us with a framed copy of the poem, which we have included at the end of this book.

After that, it was a little tough trying to compose ourselves so we could perform.

By our tenth anniversary Jamboree in 1997 we were getting a little weary of all the work involved. We continued to call it our 'friendly reunion' and our

Smilin' Johnnie

Smilin' Johnnie and Eleanor entertain at one of their jamborees at the homestead on the stage that Johnnie built himself. The flags were donated by the provincial governments across the country, as well as the Canadian and the U.S. federal governments.

friends and family came every year to enjoy the two days of fun and music.

In 1999 our youngest son, John, came to the Jamboree. We had only seen him a couple of times since his mom, my second wife, took him away when he was seven-years-old. He invited us to his wedding in Edmonton, where he lives. We arranged a number of shows in the Edmonton area and John and his wife Kim came to see us. It was a great reunion – lots of things to talk about. Lots of catching up to do. It was memorable. It was moving. This was a big step for my son to take and we are so glad that he chose to include his Dad on his wedding day. I still get choked up when I think of all those years we were apart – missing all those years when he was growing up. Not being at school concerts. Not tucking him in at night. Now he is back in my life and I am blessed.

Smilin' Johnnie

Eleanor with John Jr's wife, Kim.

Eleanor not only sings, handles the mail, makes the stage costumes, she also made the signs for the jamborees, including the one (top left) over the stage for the 50th anniversary and the one above which was placed on the roadside.

Son Bob Lucky taking care of business, selling tickets at the gate.

Smilin' Johnnie

Uncle Joe Galye, right, with Mom Lucki and two of her sisters Maggie Galye and Kate Slone.

Smilin' Johnnie with his grandson Zachary.

Smilin' Johnnie plays the bed-panjo made by Frank Stoyka of Pinewood, Ontario. Frank and Johnnie became friends after one of Johnnie's shows in Emo, Ontario.

Eleanor and Smilin' Johnnie with Zachary.

Smilin' Johnnie

Smilin' Johnnie and Eleanor have a number of stage suits. This one is bright red featuring motifs of the beloved prairie symbol - the grain elevator.

46

Yours for a smile
– Smilin' Johnnie

I hope you've found this book interesting, informative, and perhaps, eye-opening. I hope you have had the kind of enjoyment reading about my life that I have had living it!

It is without prejudice that I write this, and the names mentioned are there not to embarrass anyone. It would be impossible to compile a 60-year autobiography of being on the road and not mention names and places. Without names and places the book and its contents would be worthless!

All the people mentioned gave me more incentive to carry on. I do not have any qualms or quarrels with the entertainers, society, broadcasting or government. And the union . . . well, I guess we'll never see eye to eye. I just wish that there could be some way for those like me who don't believe in unions to be able to have opportunities to showcase their talent without having to sign a union card.

My folks have long since passed on, but I want to mention them one last time. There are not enough words to thank my parents for all they did for me - as a child and as an adult. They treated me very well, perhaps a lot better than I deserved. My folks have helped me in every respect - in spirit, with financial assistance, giving plenty of advice, and in just being there when I needed them.

I probably brought them more burdens than they expected or I intended. But

'Yours for a smile'

Smilin' Johnnie's family at the homestead in 2005 to help celebrate his 80th birthday. From left, Cheri, Bob, Tamara, Zachary, Morgan, Eleanor, Smilin' Johnnie, Rachel, Sue and Jerry. Inset is John Jr. and his wife, Kim, who were not able to make the party due to work commitments.

they were always there. Firm by my side.

When things started crumbling in 1950 and several years after, they would say, 'Johnnie, leave that crazy music.' They were only thinking of my welfare, but something in me said 'I'll just try it one more year!'

I've covered Canada in detail, and I can honestly say, that I know this country better than my own back yard (perhaps because I never got to spend much time in my backyard).

I've brought entertainment to people who had never seen 'outside' entertainment until we stepped off the airplane.

We've also played our show for low prices and sometimes we even played for nothing. We've operated as a business. Some days you make money, some days you don't, but you are always working.

You do not close down a store just because you don't get a customer during one day. This is the way I've operated the band. This method has made it possible for me to remain in business these past 60 years, good years and bad.

Many young people starting out - and even some older people who have been

Smilin' Johnnie

Following in his grandfather's footsteps - Zachary plays his toy guitar at a jamboree. Mom Lucki is under the umbrella. Zachary today plays in a high school gospel group.

in the music business - ask me what the secret is to being on the road this long. Frankly, I don't think there is a secret . . . You must make up your mind what you are going to do, and do it . . . You must never turn back, but always work to get ahead. Your brain is your biggest source of power, use it. Don't feel sorry for yourself. Don't always think about getting something for nothing, but about giving your best for the best - and fairest - price.

I never made a lot of money. In fact, most of the years we operated in the red. There were many times I could have declared bankruptcy, but that wouldn't have solved anything except get rid of a few bills. Then what?

So I chose to carry on the best I could, hoping each year for some sign, some break, some encouragement, some money in the bank.

I don't think there are others who will follow our kind of life. I can recommend it, but it does take a certain kind of person to be able to live from one job to the next, one day to the next, never putting any money in the bank, never putting money away in investments or pensions for the retirement years.

For me there will not be a retirement. We are not doing 250 or 300 shows a

'Yours for a smile'

Smilin' Johnnie with his friend **Peter Free**, who loaned him this truck for a several show dates in the Red Deer-Stettler area of Alberta when his own vehicle was in the garage for repairs. Peter, from Sunnybrook, Alberta, a friend for many years, took the photo of Smilin' Johnnie and Eleanor on the cover of this book.

year as we were way back when, but we don't turn down jobs today. We are still packed and ready to go when the telephone rings and someone wants us to play.

My comments would not be complete without a heart-felt thank-you to all my children – Jerry, Bob, John Jr., and Tammy and their loved ones, who have always supported me in doing what I love to do.

Believe me, kids, I probably cried myself to sleep at nights as much – if not more – than you did when we were apart and especially when we were parted.

I can never thank you enough and I can't find the special words it takes to express my feelings for each of you. I am truly proud of you all. I love each one of you as much as a Dad could love his children and to this day I still miss you when we are not together.

While our lives, forever entwined, are being lived in communities hundreds of miles from each other, a day doesn't go by that I don't think about each of you. I am very thankful for the happiness you all bring into my life.

And now, permit me to pay a special tribute to my wife, business partner, stage partner, companion and best friend, Eleanor Dahl.

Smilin' Johnnie

She has been a breath of fresh air all along. She has seen clearly, first-hand the problems facing the music business in Canada, and has dedicated 45 years of her life to serving the Canadian entertainment industry.

Eleanor joined me with her Dad, George Dahl, and stayed with the business even though she had seen the way the musicians would handle themselves and especially the way they treated me. She'd heard them say that I couldn't sing or play and that I was a crook and a cheat. On many occasions she'd seen me on stage singing, playing, smiling, even with a hole in the seat of my pants.

Smilin' Johnnie's daughter Tamara and her husband, Doug.

She knew that on many occasions my stomach was empty and she also knew that I often played with my eyes glued to the door, just waiting for the next bill collector to appear. Many times she saw me drive miles and miles while the rest of them slept and she knew that after the money was divided, I probably had less than anyone else.

I often told her it was time to quit. But Eleanor usually said, "There must be a way we can make a living at this."

Being younger and more talented, she felt there was a chance for her talents to be displayed and she wasn't about to quit. I often think that working with me in the early years, after seeing me kicked around like a football by business, society, radio and musicians, must not have been an easy task for her.

Nor was it an easy task for her to convince me "everything's gonna be all right.

Smilin' Johnnie

We'll win in the ninth inning!"

As we drove miles and miles across this country, Eleanor and I would discuss the pros and cons of the music business, she kept insisting that there must be a way.

I often think if only my first group in 1947 would have stuck to music as faithfully as Eleanor has, we could have been on top.

Eleanor has been with me in the music business for 45 of my 60 years on the road. She has seen me from every aspect - over-eating, starving, happy, mad, glad, sad, broke, or with a pocket full of money.

She sure has been able to make us a great team – as husband and wife and as business partners and stage partners.

We're together every single hour of every single day. We both like it like that. Neither of us would have it any other way. We're each other's best friend.

I think it is safe to say that without Eleanor, Smilin' Johnnie would have stopped performing years ago.

You've all heard the saying that behind every successful man there is a very special woman. That could have been written specifically for Eleanor.

Thank-you, Eleanor.

And I'll sign off now with the words I always use when signing my autograph:

Yours for a Smile,

Smilin' Johnnie

Smilin' Johnnie

Eleanor stitches the number 60 on the lapels of one of Smilin' Johnnie's stage suits.

47

ELEANOR'S CLOSING COMMENTS

By Eleanor Dahl

The radio is playing *On The Road Again,* while I stand at the kitchen sink, washing the breakfast dishes – I'm thinking – been there! Done that!

Don't get me wrong, it was a GREAT and unique experience that I would do all over again, if I could, but at this stage in my life, I don't long for it.

There was a time – some 45 years ago – when the mere sight of a big, old Cadillac loaded down with instruments and musicians, leaving the city, caused me to quit the relative 'security' of my office job to go 'on the road.'

I've loved every minute of it, and have absolutely NO regrets. But neither do I have anything to prove!

Looking at the World Through a Windshield was great. But, I kinda like what I see through my kitchen window – the trees we've planted around what Dad Lucky called a "happy yard." It's a whole new perspective.

Then the telephone rings, a voice says, "This is Noah calling from the 'great white north.' It takes me right back to travel and entertaining.

Johnnie comes in from clearing snow in the yard. He and Noah have a long conversation, after which we're talking about how great it would be to go north again.

Smilin' Johnnie

Eleanor in 1964

Who'da thunk it? We're once again ready to pack our bags and instruments to visit with the folks who always treated us so well.

One of the great benefits of this life of travel was seeing our country. Not many people have the opportunity to get so up close and personal with Canada.

I have always loved musing over maps, wondering 'who lives there and how does that countryside look?' Now I know.

Travelling north was especially challenging and rewarding. I'm sorry now, that, although I talked to folks at Alert, NWT, we were never able to arrange a show there.

The parkas we bought in Povungnituk, Quebec, are still with us - a little worn, but they bring back many wonderful memories.

It's such a thrill when we get calls to come back and entertain in the north. We always thought that after we toured there others would follow. But, as far as I know, it hasn't happened.

Northern travel was costly, and we bit our fingernails, hoping that we'd have enough at the end of the trip to pay expenses. But the people were so friendly and it was such a thrill to see the country. You can't put a dollar figure on these things – they're priceless.

Johnnie is a visionary who thrives on challenges – and there are plenty of them right here in the yard. He's had to learn rudimentary carpentry – building a stage for the Jamboree, while I learned to paint signs.

Eleanor's closing comments

We truly enjoyed the Jamboree part of our lives. But before we had the first one I was nearly as concerned about the financial end of things as I was the first time we flew to the Arctic and I thought we'd have to stay there the rest of our lives to pay for the airplane charter.

Weather was our biggest problem at the Jamborees. We struggled through rain storms, electrical storms and wind. We always admired the folks who stayed to watch the show in spite of the weather.

Friends from all across the country came to visit. It was great to be able to return their hospitality. They've always been so kind to us wherever we went. It was our turn to pay them back.

Of course, everyone pitched in to help us put on the show, so I don't know who benefited most.

Eleanor with her accordion in 1951 as a new teenager on the family farm at Lintlaw.

We sure loved having the folks here. They became just like 'family' and when the last trailer pulled out of the yard, we cried as if the kids had all left home.

After so many years going down the road side-by-side we feel a little lost alone! When Johnnie takes the car to be serviced, he asks me to come along. I have things I could do at home, but it's more important to be together.

Smilin' Johnnie

If I stayed home I'd be wondering how things were with him, so I might as well be there with him.

It doesn't seem right when one of us is missing. The house is empty when I am alone, and Johnnie says the car is empty if I'm not there.

At a church festival several years ago, they asked for someone to lead a sing-a-long. Both Johnnie and I got up to volunteer. It never entered our heads that they only wanted one person! Hey, we're a matched set, what can I say!

We met a couple of entertainers years back,

Eleanor, before her first birthday, with her Mom, Evelyn. The photograph was taken at the farm of Evelyn's parents (Charlie and Mary Erickson), five miles south-west of Lintlaw.

and when we asked for their address they said they didn't have one. They just travelled from place to place as they got jobs.

That amazed me. We've always been rooted someplace. I cannot imagine not having a home base.

Our present home base – *Eight Miles North and One Mile East of Wroxton,* brought Johnnie full circle. . . . and it's not too different from where I grew up at Lintlaw.

Thanks to Mom and Dad Lucky, who said "we have these few acres in our will for you, but we don't have to die to give it to you!" We are back to our roots!

It's been good for us, coming at a time in life when folks tend to become couch potatoes, we have to get out and tend to the yard – clear snow or mow grass, there's always something to do.

Both of us had to re-learn things about gardening. But now we are just as

Eleanor's closing comments

Smilin' Johnnie, Eleanor and Guy Coderre at Winnipeg Airport in 1963 when they were on a photo shoot for their first album *Treasured Country Favourites*.

thrilled with a good crop of potatoes as we are if we'd just recorded a new song.

Saskatchewan is home – whether we view it from the window of a jet, or the windshield of a Colony Park – it always looks good to us.

Home! I treasure the time we spend here. All the years of travel have been a wonderful adventure, but I'd like to have another lifetime to spend at home!

Someone once commented that our home was like a museum, not a home. I was a little miffed at the time, but now I realise he was right. It is our museum of memories. Every item, be it furniture, carvings, or pictures on the wall, takes us right back to wherever we were when we got them.

It keeps all those people and places close to us all the time. Even the houseplants remind me of Grandma, who passed on her love of growing things, to me. Having said this, though, the minute the Colony Park hits the highway, I've forgotten home and I'm focussed on the upcoming trip.

Sometimes, when we have played about five nights straight and the show comes as easy as breathing, I feel like we should just carry on – and never come back!

On the way home, however, we are just like those two old plow horses headed home after a hard day in the field – don't try to slow us down!

Smilin' Johnnie

Several years ago when our son Bob asked his Dad why he wasn't retiring, Johnnie said "and do what?" Bob said "find something you like to do and do that." Johnnie's reply was "That's what I am doing now."

I would heartily agree. It is a truly rare and wonderful privilege and blessing that God has granted me – to be able to spend my life in music and travel as I'd always dreamed.

Eleanor plays the grand piano she was given by her Dad for her sixth birthday at Lintlaw. She was about 12 when this picture was taken. The piano was traded for an upright piano when she moved to Flin Flon and the grand piano was too big for the new house.

To have shared that life with such a gentle, loving and compassionate man was the icing on the cake.

Our 'retirement' is lingering over that second cup of coffee until almost noon, then going about our daily work.

In the summertime you can find us in what we like to call 'the glass house,' where we have a couple of recliners so we can sit and watch the birds, deer or whatever else comes by while we sip our coffee and plan our day.

Many times we have thought how thankful we are to have this little piece of paradise. Not a lot of land by Saskatchewan standards, but lots of room to stretch out, relax and enjoy life.

Still – if the telephone rings in the 'glass house' and somebody wants us to come and entertain, we're quick to get things ready to leave.

My suitcase is never totally unpacked. And the equipment we take on the road is always near the station wagon in the garage.

We're always just a phone call away from leaving on the next trip.

The song creeps in again . . . about the fellow on the road . . . making music with

Eleanor's closing comments

his friends. I've always had sort of a love-hate relationship with it and I've wondered, why?

Finally, I think I know. For me, it was always about making music FOR my friends, learning about the way folks lived. Seeing the country along the road.

When I hear the song, I think, "if that was all the 'road' was about, I'd have quit a long time ago."

We've travelled to places most folks have to take expensive vacations to visit. We've met the people . . . in many cases stayed with them in their home . . . eaten at their table . . . so "just making music with my friends" sounds pretty superficial to me.

Sometimes, when the winter snow blocks

Smilin' Johnnie and Eleanor perform at the Saskatchewan Country Music Hall of Fame in 1995 at Watrous, when receiving their second Legend and Legacy Award for their contribution to the music scene in Saskatchewan. The presentation was made by Trudy Vipond, the person responsible for starting the Saskatchewan Country Music Hall of Fame. Their first Legend and Legacy Award in 1993 was presented by Harry Dekker, manager of CJNB Radio Station in North Battleford who got to know Smilin' Johnnie when he was the resident band 30 years before. Harry, Smilin' Johnnie and Eleanor remained friends over the years.

that "One mile East" that separates our little yard from the highway which represents the 'road', I'm quite content . . . secure . . . knowing that – at least for now – I won't have to pack and leave . . . at least not until the snow plow comes to open the way to the 'road.'

Eleanor Dahl

March 2006

226

Smilin' Johnnie

Smilin' Johnnie and Eleanor Dahl have written and recorded dozens of their own songs, including many gospel songs. They always end their show with a hymn. On the following pages are some of the positive songs that have made them popular with audiences across the country.

When we walk with Jesus

When we walk with Jesus
And embrace him as our friend
Asking him to help us
To our needs he will attend

At peace

(By Eleanor)
God tells us his way will bring true peace
Why don't we give it a try
All else has failed over 6,000 years
Surely God's way could never be worse
Obey his laws and see what transpires
We'll find that it works for God is no liar

Stay close to God

Stay close to God to the one who gives
life
Stay close to God he's Eternal our guide
Stay close in thought and in action as
well
Stay close to God to the giver of life

The power of prayer

The power of prayer to God and Jesus
The power of prayer will give us ease
The power of prayer to God is soothing
The power of prayer will give us peace

Let's praise our God

Let's praise our God and let's all praise
his name
Let's praise our God for it is he who
has the fame
He is always ready and waiting
How merciful and scintillating
Yes, let's praise our God and let's all
praise his name

God's written word

God's written words are the words of
truth
God's written words no one can dispute
God's written words may be read and
be heard
The words of life are in his word

Smilin' Johnnie

Smilin' Johnnie and Eleanor have written many songs offering advice for a happy life. Astum is a word well known among first nations people.

Let's be polite

It's the simple things in life
The decisions that we make
Can bring us joy or make us sad
Depends what path we take

Out in the public we should try
To let our examples shine
Through our kindness and respect
To everyone we find

It's not nice

It's not nice to point your finger

It's not nice to wag your tongue

It's not nice to pursue gossip

It's not nice you know it's wrong

Astum

Astum was the one word that she said

Astum meant come here you were so bad

It means you don't persuade

You say astum it's obeyed

And astum was the magic word she had

Enjoy a happy life

To each day just bring a sparkle

With a kind and pleasant way

Let love be shown to others

Never turning them away

Add a smile

Life's not always easy
Many times it's cruel rough
But the way to overcome it
Is be positive and tough

Just take time

Our life's journey needs to be adjusted

From time to time as we see time fly

We need to know when to speed up when to slow down

Have the balance use it wisely always try

Let's take the time

Let's take the time to make life happy

Let's take the time to do things well

And when you do aim for perfection

Let's take the time always excel

Smilin' Johnnie

Smilin' Johnnie and Eleanor love to put their feelings into song for special events

60 years in music

Sixty years in music and travelling on the road

Taking entertainment to all the folks around

Sixty years of singing and harmonizing too

Bringing joy to others is what we love to do

Give the roses

Give the roses when she can smell them

Give the roses when she can see

Bring a flower when it's in blossom

'twill leave such a happy memory

I was always here

I was always here

I wanted to see you so much

As time was drawing near

I was always waiting

To hear from you each and every day

I remind myself of you

I remind myself of you

In everything I do

But there's one thing for sure

I remind myself of you

Forty Acre plot

It's that 40 acre plot

May not seem like a lot

It's open and so free

A lot of room for you and me

While on this earth

While on this earth I'd like to see you

While on this earth I'd like you here

To talk to you and smile with you

While on this earth and while I am here

For when I'm gone I won't be talking

When I am gone there will be no smile

When I am gone I won't be seeing

All the flowers you'll bring in style

We're only here for a visit

We're only here for a visit

We're only here for a while

We're put here to be perfected

And we all must walk that mile

Smilin' Johnnie

Some of Smilin' Johnnie and Eleanor's songs about a few of the places they love

Up North

For up north is the place you'll want to be

The place where so many go to see

Oh, there's hunting, whaling, fishing

And I know that you'll be wishing

To stay up north in the land of liberty

I'm going north

I'm going north I love the north

And going north gives me a pleasure

I am going north I love the north

For going north is a trip that I treasure

Call of the north

Call of the north is for you my dear

The call of the north come join us here

We're waiting for you don't make us feel blue

The call of the north is especially for you

Eight Miles North

Eight miles north and one mile east of Wroxton

To where the fresh air flows

Eight miles north and one mile east of Wroxton

Is where the quack grass grows

Where the sun shines so brightly

And the birds sing so sweetly

You know where that is done

It's eight miles north and one mile east of Wroxton

Saskatchewan

Saskatchewan my prairie home

You call to me where 'ere I roam

Saskatchewan from prairie to pine

The home I will always call mine

Stony Creek Waltz

Where the clear water flows

And the breeze softly blows

Where natures beauty never halts

Where the flowers all sway

Just as much as to say

Watch us dance to the Stony Creek Waltz

Smilin' Johnnie

Smilin' Johnnie's answer to *I've Been Everywhere*. He literally draws circles on a map and tries to play a number of shows within that area to make the trip economical.

Drawing Circles on the map

Drawing circles on the map

Looking where all we have been

Where we've travelled, where we've played

And all the people we have seen

From Jaffray to Old Crow to Tuktoyaktuk

From Greenwood to Skidegate to Holman Island

From Youbou to Puntzi Mountain to Dawson City

From Buffalo to Edson to Fort Vermilion

From Killdeer to Chipewyan to Rae and Yellowknife

Alida to Coppermine to Buffalo Narrows

Pierson to Wabowden to Rankin Inlet

From Barwick to Easterville to Osnaburgh House

From Lansdowne to Moosonee on to Fort Albany

Fort George to Sugluk to Frobisher Bay

From Almonte to Lennoxville to Richibucto

Knowlton, Mistissini to Povungnituk

St. Martins to Gaspe, Sussex on to Hartland

Moncton to Summerside, Tignish and Souris

Barrington to Cheticamp to Petit de Grat

From Deer Lake to Carbonear on to Grand Bank

Smilin' Johnnie

Smilin' Johnnie and Eleanor have written many love songs

The Last Three Words

The last three words should be loving

The last three words should be true

As you leave don't forget this adieu

The last three words should be I Love You

Each day

Each day we are together

Is a day we're not apart

Each day we are together

Brings you closer to my heart

I'll hold your hand

I'll hold your hand though your face grows wrinkled

I'll hold your hand though your hair turns grey

As we get older love grows stronger along the way

I'll hold your hand and love you still day after day

Before I forget

Before I forget to be pleasant

And be cheerful so I won't regret

When the day passes by there's no returning

Oh, please help me so I don't forget

Fully in love

Fully in love feels so nice

A beautiful way to sacrifice

Fully in love feels so great

Sure makes life easy to celebrate

It's so easy

(wrote for my wife)

It's so easy to love you

It's so easy to care

Whenever I need you

I know that you'll be there

Smilin' Johnnie

The following song was written by Johnnie and Eleanor in response to many people asking them, 'how long can you continue to sing and perform?' Usually Johnnie writes the words and Eleanor creates the music. On this song they both wrote the words and music.

But until then

CHORUS
BUT UNTIL THEN WE'LL BOTH KEEP ON SINGING
YES UNTIL THEN WE'LL BE WITH YOU A WHILE
WE THANK YOU ALL FOR COMING OUT TO SEE US
YES, UNTIL THEN WE'LL TRAVEL, SING AND SMILE

WHEN LIFE BEGAN OUR HEARTS WERE FULL OF SINGING
AS TIME WENT BY ALL THINGS BEGAN TO CHANGE
THESE EARTHLY THINGS DID DIM AND LOSE THEIR VALUE
FOR THEY WERE ONLY BORROWED FOR A WHILE

AS WE GO ON LIFE TAKES A DIFFERENT MEANING
THIS WAY OF LIFE IS WHAT WE LOVE TO DO
UNTIL THE DAY OUR EYES BEHOLD THE SAVIOUR
THIS TROUBLED WORLD IS NOT OUR FINAL HOME

Smilin' Johnnie Shows
Box 190-210, Wroxton,
Saskatchewan, S0A 4S0
Phone: (306) 742-4356
CD, LP, Cassette & Souvenir

#1 Best of Smilin' Johnnie – Johnnie and Eleanor sing *I Want to Live*, *Lure of the Arctic*, *Saskatchewan*, *Poison in Your Hands*, *They Leave You So Soon* and more. O T

#2 Instrumentals – A collection of music featuring Eleanor on accordion & piano; Guy Coderre on guitar & fiddle; Lawrence Bourgeois on guitar & fiddle. Jigs, Heel 'n' Toe, etc. O T

#3 Accordion Selections – Eleanor plays "old-time" tunes; foxtrots, waltz's and polkas with Johnnie on rhythm guitar. O T

#4 Piano Selections – Eleanor plays a collection of old standards and some original compositions. O T

#5 A Touch of Scandinavian & Ukrainian – Johnnie & Eleanor play Swedish waltzes, schottisches and hambos with 3 songs in Ukrainian. O T

#6 Songs as You Requested – Johnnie and Eleanor sing *Faded Love*, *Storms Never Last*, *Tennessee Waltz* and more. T

#7 On the Road – The Smilin' Johnnie Show recorded live with songs, music, comedy by Olga the Janitor as well as Hymn time. O T

#8 Quiet Time – Johnnie and Eleanor sing hymns, gospel songs and some original inspirational songs like *Just a Closer Walk With Thee* and *According to the Bible*. O T

#9 More Country Favourites – a collection of songs, some from our Northern album, the "B" side features the Inuit of Povungnetuk singing a hymn for us. O T

#10 Good Old Songs – 20's – includes *Wreck of the Old '97*, *Prisoner's Song*, *Little Green Valley*, *Cowboy Jack* and more. T

#11 Good Old Songs – 20's & 30's – includes *Letter Edged in Black*, *Red River Valley*, *Silver Haired Daddy of Mine* and more. T

#12 Good Old Songs - 30's & 40's – includes *Wabash Cannon Ball*, *Makes*

Smilin' Johnnie

No Difference Now, Be Honest With Me and more. T

#13 Good Old Songs – 40's – includes *You Are My Sunshine, Rose of San Antone, Let the Rest of the World Go By* and more. T

#14 Good Old Songs – 40's – includes *Mexicali Rose, Nobody's Darlin' But Mine, Bouquet of Roses* and more. T

#15 Good Old Songs – 40's & 50's - includes *Happy Roving Cowboy, Little Red Wagon, Tears On My Pillow* and more. T

#16 Remembrance of the 50's – songs & violin tunes recorded by Eleanor's dad, George Dahl during the '50's. It includes Eleanor at age 16 or 17. In the 1990's she added piano accompaniment. O T

#17 Our Kind of Country – Johnnie and Eleanor's original songs – *Saskatchewan, Cabin by the Peace* and more. O

#18 Reflections - Original songs by Johnnie & Eleanor – *Empty Pockets, 50 Years From Now* and more with steel guitar and electric bass. O

#19 Comedy Thru the Years – Various comedy skits by various performers who were in the show over the years.

#20 Many Years Ago – Featuring Eleanor Dahl and her dad, George. Fiddle by dad and piano by Eleanor recorded live many years ago. T

#21 Memories of the CJNB Years – Actual radio shows recorded in the early 60's featuring the singing and playing of Johnnie, Eleanor, Guy Coderre, Luke Jeddry and George Dahl. T

#22 Sweet Harmony – includes *Ashes of Love, Mr. & Mrs. Used To Be, Just Between the Two of Us* and more. T

#23 Remember Me – includes *One by One, Remember Me, Soft Rain, When My Blue Moon Turns to Gold Again* and more. T

#24 Looking Back Together – includes *You and Me, I Walk Alone, Lookin' Back to See, Are You Teasin' Me?* and more. T

#25 Just For Fun – includes *Slap 'er Down Again, Out Behind the Barn, How to Make Love* and more. T

#26 Spreading Sunshine – featuring all original tunes like *Don't Pretend, Poor Broke Farmer* and more. O

#27 Quiet Time II – inspirations songs like *It is No Secret, The Man Upstairs, Rose Upon the Bible, Beyond the Sunset* and more. O T

#28 We Weren't Always Country – 15 instrumental tunes like *Sweet Georgia Brown, At Sundown, The West* and more. Includes 2 vocals by Eleanor and Johnnie with Ray McNeil's B♭ saxophone. T

#29 Easy Listening & Dancing Waltzes – 16 instrumentals like *Accordion Waltz, Let me Call You Sweetheart, Smile Awhile* and more. Eleanor on accordion, Johnnie on guitar and Ray on sax. T

#30 Tribute to Keray Regan – Johnnie and Eleanor sing songs written and recorded by their friend Keray Regan. Includes *My Home by the Fraser, Poor, Poor Farmer, The Poplar Tree* and more. O

#31 More Good Old Songs – includes *Coat of Many Colors, Release Me, Signed Sealed and Delivered* and more. T

#32 Give Us This Day – original songs with words by Johnnie and music by Eleanor. Includes *Each Day, Maybe Today* and more. O

#33 Quiet Time III – More Gospel songs like *Amazing Grace, Will the Circle be Unbroken, I've Got a Mansion* and more. T

#34 More Requests – Their most requested songs like *I'll Be All Smiles, Silver Threads Among the Gold, True and Trembling Brakeman* and more. T

#35 50 Years – Johnnie , Eleanor and friends perform *It's Not Nice, I Was Always Here, 8 Miles North & 1 Mile East (of Wroxton)* and more. O

#36 Golden Western – Recorded on Johnnie's 50th and Eleanor's 35th Anniversary in the music industry featuring *Whispering Hope, Tumbling Tumbleweeds, I'm Bitin' My Fingernails* and more. T

#37 Our Recollections – Collection of original songs featuring Ray McNeil on saxophone.

LP's or Authorized Cassette Copies Available:

CML-1064 Treasured Country Favorites – copy of our first long-playing record – with Guy Coderre on lead guitar and fiddle.

CML-1065 Salute to Canada's Northland – original songs and instrumentals with Johnnie, Eleanor & Guy Coderre. (Also on LP)

CML-1066 Smilin Johnnie Show in Action – Johnnie, Eleanor & Guy Coderre, with comedy by "Charlie" – recorded live in Yellowknife, NWT. (Also on LP)

CML-1067 Happy Musical Moments – Johnnie, Eleanor & Lawrence Bourgeois sing and play original songs and instrumentals including Saskatchewan & the Ukrainian Song.

CML-1068 Rollin' Along – Johnnie, Eleanor & Guy Coderre sing and play songs like *Candy Kisses*, *As Long As I Live* and more. (Also on LP)

CML-1070 Twenty-Five Years – a 60 Minute Cassette (or 2 LP's) featuring ALL original songs by Johnnie & Eleanor plus a back-up band. Johnnie talks about his 25 years in music on the "B" side.

CML-1071 Watchin' Our Country Die – another ALL original recording featuring Johnnie & Eleanor with a band.

No longer available on LP.

CML-1072 Cattle Collection – features songs from the above LP. This is a copy of an LP that was produced and sold in West Germany. No longer available on LP.

CD's Available:

#1 Understandable Country I – a collection of original songs taken from various sources.

#2 Twenty-Five Years – a copy of our two-LP set which was recorded for Johnnie's 25th year in music.

#3 Understandable Country II – a 2nd collection of original songs.

#4 Understandable Country III – a 3rd collection of original songs.

#5 Traditional Country – a collection of songs recorded for cassettes #22, 23, 24 & 36.

#6 Old Time Gospel I – a collection of gospel songs which were featured on various cassettes #8, 27 & 33.

#7 Old Time Gospel II – more gospel favorites taken from various cassettes and LP's.

#8 Simply Country – many country favorites from days gone by.

#9 We Weren't Always Country – a collection of instrumentals recorded with Ray McNeil playing saxophone.

#10 Easy Listening & Dancing – a collection of waltzes recorded with Ray McNeil playing saxophone.

#11 Happy Musical Moments/Salute to Canada's Northland – a CD copy of those two LP recordings.

#12 Rollin' Along/Watchin' Our Country Die? – a CD copy of those two LP recordings.

#13 Our Recollections – a collection of original songs, from our most recent cassette, as well as selections from earlier releases.

Video Tape Recordings Available:

VHS-#1 – complete 2-hour stage show recorded live at Bradwell, Saskatchewan, plus various TV interviews. $49.95

VHS-#2 – complete 3 hour 50th Anniversary show recorded live at St. Gerard's Auditorium, Yorkton, SK plus various TV interviews. $49.95

VHS-#3 – The Smilin' Johnnie & Eleanor Dahl show recorded live at Watson, SK.

VHS-#4 – The Smilin' Johnnie & Eleanor Dahl show recorded live March 2002 in Yorkton, SK.

Books Available:

Eight Miles North and One Mile East of Wroxton by Smilin' Johnnie. Johnnie writes about 60 years in the music business in Canada. This is 240 pages of stories of life on the road, the good times and the bad. Being a musician is not always as glamorous as it seems. Soft cover $25.00 plus $7 postage.

Eight Miles North and One Mile East of Wroxton by Smilin' Johnnie. Johnnie writes about 60 years in the music business in Canada. This is 240 pages of stories of life on the road, the good times and the bad. Being a musician is not always as glamorous as it seems. Hard cover $37.5 plus $10 postage.

T-Shirts & Miscellaneous Souvenirs Available:
- T-Shirts in Large or Xtra-Large - $18.00
- T-Shirts in XXL - $20.00
- Caps - $7.00
- 8x10 Colour Photos - $5.00

Price List:
Cassettes
$13 each or
2 for $25
4 for $50
9 for $100

CDs $20 each
or
6 for $100

Please include
$5 for postage

Smilin' Johnnie prepares to fulfill another order for his CDs.

Send orders to:
Smilin' Johnnie Shows
Box 190-210
Wroxton, SK
S0A 4S0

A LEGEND IN YOUR TIME

Smilin' Johnnie, as we all know
Started in music, a long time ago.
To entertain folks, for miles around
A man more determined, cannot be found.

Summer or Winter, whatever the condition
To put on a good show, was their greatest ambition.
Johnnie and Eleanor, make a good team
They both pull together, ahead at full steam.

Singing and playing, they love every minute
Not only because, of the money that's in it.
If you had a choice, would you play the same game
Certainly would, we'd do it all over again.

They've traveled the highways, and also by plane
To remote parts of Canada, just to entertain.
Johnnie and Eleanor, have their own style
To see people smile, to them it's worthwhile.

They're always on time, for all their shows
Just how they manage, God only knows.
At times it must be hard, it goes without sayin'
It's not that easy, to just keep on playin'.

Johnnie's Jamboree, where friends get together
Good music, fellowship, and memories forever.
Johnnie and Eleanor, however happy you seem
I think it's because, you have lived a dream.

You deserve a lot of credit, for what you're still doing
I could not have endured, and I'm not fooling.
To etch out a living, doing just that
To you Johnnie and Eleanor, I take off my hat.

Lawrence Zelionka

Eleanor's favourite picture of Smilin' Johnnie.

Lawrence Zelionka wrote this poem to honour his frieind, Smilin' Johnnie. Lawrence is with his wife, Dorothy, on the dance floor at one of Smilin' Johnnie's jamborees

ISBN 141208912-3